LANGUAGE!®

The Comprehensive Literacy Curriculum

Jane Fell Greene, Ed.D.

SOPRIS WEST EDUCATIONAL SERVICES
A CAMBIUM LEARNING COMPANY

BOSTON, MA • NEW YORK, NY • LONGMONT, CO

Editorial Director: Nancy Chapel Eberhardt
Word and Phrase Selection: Judy Fell Woods
English Learners: Jennifer Wells Greene
Lesson Development: Sheryl Ferlito, Donna Lutz, Isabel Wesley
Morphology: John Alexander, Mike Minsky, Bruce Rosow
Text Selection: Sara Buckerfield, Jim Cloonan
Decodable and Independent Text: Jenny Hamilton, Steve Harmon

LANGUAGE! eReader is a customized version of the
CAST eReader for Windows® (3.0). CAST eReader
©1995—2003, CAST, Inc. and its licensors. All rights reserved.

ISBN 1-59318-321-6

Printed in the United States of America

Published and distributed by

SOPRIS
WEST
EDUCATIONAL SERVICES

4093 Specialty Place • Longmont, CO 80504 • (303) 651-2829
www.sopriswest.com

*"I'm proud that I'm pushing myself to be better.
I love learning and I don't ever want to stop improving."*

—Fabiola da Silva (1979–)

Table of Contents

This book contains six units.

Each unit builds knowledge in:

- Sounds and Letters
- Spelling and Words
- Vocabulary and Roots
- Grammar and Usage
- Listening and Reading
- Speaking and Writing

Unit 13 Invent It

Unit 15 Be a Hero

Unit 16 Cheer an Athlete

Go to Egypt

Appendix

Explore a Continent

STEP 1

Phonemic Awareness and Phonics

Unit 18 reviews the syllable types learned so far in Books A–C.

Syllable Types

Review: Words are made up of syllables.

- A syllable is a word part that has one vowel sound.
- Every word has at least one syllable.
- The syllable type is determined by the syllable's vowel sound.

Syllable Type	Pattern	Vowel Sound	Diacritical Mark
Closed	A syllable that ends with a consonant sound. (**dig, trans-mit**)	The vowel sound is short.	ă
r-Controlled	A syllable that has a vowel followed by **r**. (**car, mar**-ket)	The vowel sound is r-controlled: / âr /, / ôr /, or / êr /.	âr
Open	A syllable that ends with a vowel. (**she, my, o**-pen)	The vowel sound is long.	ā
Final silent e	A syllable that ends in a final silent **e** (**made**, in-**flate**)	The vowel sound is long.	ā_e

2 Word Recognition and Spelling

Syllables

Review: We put vowels and consonants together to make **syllables**. Every word has at least one vowel sound, so every word has at least one syllable. The number of syllables equals the number of vowel sounds.

> **Syllables**
>
> 1 vowel = 1 syllable: cab
>
> 2 vowels = 2 syllables: cab + in = cabin
>
> 3 vowels = 3 syllables: cab + in + et = cabinet

Prefixes and Suffixes

We can build longer words and change their meaning by adding **prefixes** and **suffixes**.

- Prefixes are added to the beginning of words.
- Suffixes are added to the end of words.

Refer to page 247 for a list of prefixes and their meanings.

Words With Prefixes and Suffixes

antidote	intertwine	subdivide	undergo
antilock	nonmagnetic	subnormal	underline
antimatter	pretend	supertanker	undertake
contact	prevent	supervise	unexplored
contest	reenter	translate	unfinished
distribute	refinish	transport	uninterested
inflame	relocate	underdone	unopened

Compound Words

Compound words are words made up of two or more smaller words. In a compound word, both words have to be real words that can stand on their own. Example: birth + day = birthday

Compound Word Review

anybody	itself	pathway	sunset
baseline	lifelike	pipeline	together
birthday	lonesome	something	understand
dateline	maybe	sometimes	upset
fireside	outside	sunrise	yourself

Essential Words

Essential Words are the words we use most often when we speak, read, or write. Unit 18 focuses on 20 for review.

Essential Word Review

again	people	though	too
answer	poor	through	two
certain	their	to	want
gone	there	today	what
laugh	they	tomorrow	who

All **Essential Words** for Books A, B, and C appear on page 201.

Spelling Lists

The Unit 18 spelling lists contain four word categories:

1. Words with closed, r-controlled, open, and final silent **e** syllables

2. Compound words

3. Words with learned prefixes and suffixes

4. **Essential Words** (in italics)

Spelling Lists

Lessons 1–5		Lessons 6–10	
answer	*to*	antilock	problem
hammer	*too*	brother	tornado
open	*two*	exploring	tried
people	upset	maybe	relocated
remote	*what*	music	report
symbols	*want*	outside	translate
their	*who*	pathway	understand
there		pipeline	

Vocabulary and Morphology

Unit Vocabulary

Sound-spelling correspondences and syllable types from this unit and previous units make up this unit's vocabulary.

- What do these words mean?

- Do some of them mean more than one thing? Which ones?

UNIT Vocabulary

after	discovered	happened	normal	smart
alone	divine	harvest	number	spotted
arrived	entered	inflate	only	squirrel
body	explode	insects	perfume	stampede
brother	exploring	interesting	planets	students
burning	extreme	letter	plaster	summer
canine	factors	linked	polite	supplies
canyon	farmers	living	primary	symbols
carpet	feline	located	problem	thinning
contact	fever	market	products	tornado
continent	fingers	members	remote	traffic
corner	finished	menu	report	trapped
covered	first	merchants	river	tried
create	flavor	migrate	second	western
cried	gases	minutes	secrets	winter
deliver	govern	mother	sharp	wonder
diet	gravel	music	shipped	
direct	hammer	nickel	sister	

Word Relationships

Word Relationships	What Is It?	Unit 18 Examples
antonyms	Words that have opposite meanings	after/before; many/few; first/last; sunrise/sunset
synonyms	Words that have the same or a similar meaning	today/now; little/small; find/discover
homophones	Words that sound the same but have different meanings	to/two/too; their/there; I/eye
attributes	Words that tell more about the word, such as size, function, parts, color, shape, or texture	eye/lid; body/arms; minute/seconds; nickel/round

Meaning Parts

Prefixes

Prefixes can add to or change the meanings of words.

Prefixes	Meanings	Examples
non-	not; without	nonsense
pre-	before	preregister
re-	back; again	revisit

Refer to page 247 for a list of prefixes and their meanings.

Suffixes

Suffixes can change the meaning or function of words.

Verb Endings

-s or **-es**	Third person singular, present tense. Examples: dives, wishes
-ed	Past tense. Example: jumped
-ing	Progressive (on-going action) with *am, is,* or *are; was* or *were;* or *will be.* Examples: am swimming; was jumping; will be wishing

Noun Endings

-s or -es	More than one. Examples: arms, dishes
-'s or -s'	Possessive. Example: tomorrow's storm, the planets' orbits

Adjectives
Single Syllable

-er	Comparison between *two* people, places, or things (comparative). Example: She is the shorter sister.
-est	Comparison among *three or more* people, places, or things (superlative). Example: She is the shortest of my three sisters.

Multisyllable

more	Comparison of *two* people, places, or things (comparative). Example: more remote
most	Comparison of *three or more* people, places, or things (superlative). Example: the most remote

Verbs as Adjectives

-ing	The present participle of a verb may act as an adjective. Example: a driving school
-ed or -en	The past participle of a verb may act as an adjective. Examples: a tiled roof, a frozen continent

STEP 4

Grammar and Usage

Noun Function	Explanation	Unit 18 Examples
Subject	Nouns serve as the subject (S) of a sentence. The subject names the person, place, thing, or idea that the sentence is about.	The **railroad** crossed the continent.
Direct Object	Nouns can be the direct object (DO) of the sentence. The direct object is the person, place, or thing that receives the action.	The workers sent **messages**.
Indirect Object	Nouns can be the indirect object (IO) in a sentence. The indirect object is the noun or pronoun that often comes between the main verb and the direct object.	The workers sent their **families** messages.
Object of a Preposition	Nouns can be the object of a preposition (OP) in a sentence.	They built the railroad **across** the **continent**.

Nouns can have different functions in sentences. They can be the subject, direct object, indirect object, or object of a preposition.
Example: Her son gave Anna some flowers in a vase.
(son = subject; Anna = indirect object; flowers = direct object; vase = object of the preposition)

Unit 18 Nouns

brother	fireside	music	tornado
canine	hammer	pipeline	traffic
canyon	insects	planets	winter
eye	market	report	
farmers	menu	river	
fingers	mother	sister	

Verbs

A **verb** is the base of the predicate of a sentence. There are different types of verbs.

- **Action verb:** A verb that describes actions. Examples: **open**, **inflate**, **create**

- **Helping verb:** An auxiliary verb that comes before the main verb in a sentence. Helping verbs include forms of **be**, **do**, and **have**. Examples: **am** opening, **did** inflate, **have** created

Some verbs signal time through irregular verb forms.

Base Verb	Irregular Past Tense
be	was/were
become	became
begin	began
bring	brought
do	did
fly	flew
go	went
have	had
shine	shone
withstand	withstood

Compound Sentences

Review: A **compound sentence** is two sentences joined by a conjunction. The sentences are joined by the conjunctions **and**, **but**, and **or**. When combining longer sentences, place a comma before the conjunction.

> **Compound Sentence With and**
>
> Workers created the railroad across the continent.
>
> They impacted many lives.
>
> Workers created the railroad across the continent, and they impacted many lives.

In this compound sentence, *Workers created the railroad across the continent* and *they impacted many lives* are joined by the conjunction **and**. A comma is placed before **and**.

The diagram below shows how to build this compound sentence with two base sentences.

Form: N/V/N + N/V/N   **noun/verb/noun**

Function: S/P/DO + S/P/DO **subject/predicate/direct object + subject/predicate/direct object**

Workers created the **railroad** across the **continent,** **and they** impacted many **lives.**

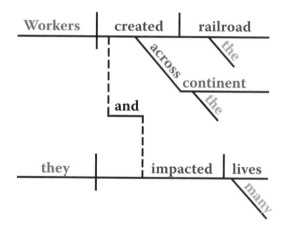

Listening and Reading Comprehension

Informational and Narrative Text

■ Some **informational** text is organized by **classification**. Ideas, facts, evidence, or examples are organized into categories. **Transition words** signal this organization. These transition words can be used within and between paragraphs.

> **Transition Words for Classification**
>
> the first kind, the second kind, another kind, the last kind
>
> the first point, the next point, the final point

Literary Terms and Devices

📖 **Figures of speech** and **literary devices** help us create images in what we read. In Unit 18, two of these are illustrated:

■ **Personification:** Figurative language that assigns human characteristics to an animal, an idea, or a thing. Examples: Elephants waltzed across the plains; The United Nations building overlooks the river. "**Continental Drift**" reviews personification.

■ **Mood:** A literary device that conveys the general emotion of a work or of the author. For example, the mood of a story might begin with words that describe excitement, change to frustration when a conflict occurs, and then turn to triumph as the story comes to a close. "**The First Transcontinental Railroad**" uses mood as a literary device.

Vocabulary in Context

■ **Context clues** help us understand new vocabulary. Pronoun referents, meaning signals, and visuals, such as pictures, charts, and graphs, provide meaning links.

Signal Words

■ To comprehend what we read and hear, we have to understand many different types of questions. Different types of questions can help us think about new information in different ways.

- **Remember It** questions ask us to recall information.
  Signal words: recognize, state, list, locate, name, recall, retrieve, repeat, describe

- **Understand It** questions ask us to put facts together to build meaning. Answers to these questions require a new organization of information.
  Signal words: predict, conclude, illustrate, define in your own words, tell, summarize, paraphrase, identify, sort, classify, categorize, match, discuss, explain, compare, contrast

- **Apply It** questions ask us to use information or procedures. Answers to these questions must explain or use information to do something.
  Signal words: generalize, infer, use, show

- **Analyze It** questions ask us to break down information and see how the parts relate in patterns and structures. Answers to these questions require an organization of information to show the relationship of parts.
  Signal words: distinguish, select, organize, outline, arrange

Refer to page 232 for a chart of the signal words for each type of question.

STEP 6

Speaking and Writing

We use different types of sentences when we speak and write.

Statements: Fact or Opinion

■ Some sentences present facts or opinions. These are called **statements**.

> **Statements**
>
> **The weather in Antarctica is dry, cold, and windy.**
> This tells us a fact about Antarctica.
> What? The weather is dry, cold, and windy.
>
> **Many people would like to visit Antarctica.**
> This expresses an opinion about people's likes.
> What? They would like to visit Antarctica.

Signal Words

■ Some sentences ask for information. They require putting information or ideas together to create an answer. They use specific **signal words**. See Step 5 for an explanation of each type of question. Refer to page 232 for a chart of the signal words.

> **Signal Words**
>
> **Describe** the weather in Antarctica.
>
> **Identify** the problems encountered while building the transcontinental railroad.
>
> **Use** information to explain how the continents were once joined.
>
> **Outline** the difficulties encountered by the railroads.

Paragraph Organization

■ Some paragraphs are organized by classification. These paragraphs include ideas, facts, evidence, or examples organized by categories. **Transition words** signal this organization. These transition words can be used within and between paragraphs. Examples: one example, another example, the final one

More About Words

- **Bonus Words** use the same sound-spelling correspondences that we have studied in this unit and previous units.

- **Idioms** are common phrases that cannot be understood by the meanings of their separate words—only by the entire phrase.

- **Why? Word History** tells us about the origin and meaning of the word *continent*.

- **Essential Words** from Books A, B, and C are included.

UNIT Bonus Words

archway	flyer	likewise	strengthen
clockwork	gangway	limestone	super
command	gateway	namesake	tiresome
define	hatchway	oneself	underwater
discover	hereby	parkway	
driveway	homework	pathway	
ego	hotel	pigpen	
entryway	lifeline	stalemate	

Idioms	
Idiom	**Meaning**
make no bones about	be forthright and candid about; acknowledge freely
make the grade	measure up to a given standard
make tracks	move or leave in a hurry
make waves	cause a disturbance or controversy
open your eyes	become aware of the truth of a situation
put to bed	make final preparations for completing a project
put two and two together	draw the proper conclusions from existing evidence or indications
put your finger on something	point out or describe exactly; find something
run like clockwork	operate with machinelike regularity and precision; perfectly
take at your word	be convinced of your sincerity and act in accord with what you say

 **Word History**

continent—*The American Heritage Dictionary,* Fourth Edition (2002), defines *continent* as: "One of the principal land masses of the earth." These are usually regarded as Africa, Antarctica, Asia, Australia, Europe, North America, and South America. The prefix *con* means "with" or "together." The root *tenere* means "to hold." So, *continent* literally means "holding together."

Originally, it meant anything that is contained (the contents). Later, it meant any body of land contained within a boundary. By 1600, the word had obtained its modern meaning.

The origin of a word is often not the same as its meaning. Meanings can change over time, but a word's origin remains the same.

Essential Words Review

a	every	now	through
about	find	of	to
again	for	oil	today
all	from	only	tomorrow
almost	gone	our	too
alone	good	out	two
already	great	people	very
also	he	poor	want
although	her	right	was
always	here	said	water
answer	how	say	way
any	I	see	we
are	into	she	were
be	is	should	what
been	know	small	when
body	laugh	sound	where
call	little	that	who
certain	look	the	why
could	many	their	word
day	may	there	work
do	me	these	would
does	most	they	write
down	Mr.	this	year
Dr.	Mrs.	those	you
each	Ms.	though	your
engine	new	thought	

Life at the Pole

A Frozen Land

The temperature is less than zero! The wind gusts at more than 200 mph. The windchill hits the danger zone. The land is frozen. Welcome to Antarctica. It is also called the South Pole. It is very dry and cold. There's
5 not much life. Small plants live on the frozen shore. Krill thrive in the cold waters. Whales migrate to the Antarctic. They come just for krill. Other forms of life come. Many birds visit, too.

A Mixed-Up Sky

At the pole, days are far from normal. In the summer,
10 there is constant day. It is never dark. Summer begins in October. It ends in March! These are winter months in the U.S. The planet tilts. This brings constant sunshine. Is it hard to go to bed? Yes. The sun is still up. Dwellings have thick shades. This makes it dark inside.
15 What is it like in winter? It is dark all the time! The planet tilts. This prevents direct sunshine. It's hard to get up in the dark. An alarm clock wakes you, not the rising sun. There is some light in the sky. It comes from gases. Swirling gases color the winter sky. To adjust takes time!

Secrets in the Land

20　　Who governs Antarctica? Many countries do. People come from all over. They come to study. They set up labs. They work to understand the planet better. They study many things. They study the thinning ozone. They study things preserved in the frozen land. Dark objects
25　are quickly spotted. They contrast with the land's white blanket. Even bits of Mars have been found! People have also found fossils. This land was not always frozen. At one time, it was part of a lush forest. It was filled with life. Life left its imprints. These are trapped in fossils.
30　Studying them helps us understand the past. A very long time ago, one landmass existed. Antarctica was part of it. All the continents were one. Fossils confirm these facts.

　　　　People do not make the Antarctic their home. They
35　come for a short time. They study. They write. They work to uncover secrets. Secrets from the past unlock the future.

A panoramic view of the South Geographic Pole with South Pole station.

Mysteries of ANTARCTICA

Antarctica is a mysterious continent. Some call it a penguin's playground. Others call it the end of the Earth. Antarctica is the home of the South Pole. Want to visit the South Pole? There, you can "walk around the world"

5   in a few steps. You can step on every time zone and **longitude** in less than a minute. Check for yourself. Look at Antarctica on a globe.

    In Antarctica, the seasons are different. They are reversed. Summer lasts from October to March. Winter

10   lasts from April to September. In the summer, daylight lasts 24 hours a day. In winter, it stays dark all day. During the dark winter months, there is often an aurora display. Green, orange, and red clouds of gas flash across the sky.

    The weather in Antarctica is very dry, cold, and windy.

15   It has the harshest climate of all the continents. It has only about three inches of snowfall each year. Antarctica has been called the frozen frontier. Just how cold is it? It's never above freezing. Only a small amount of the land is free from ice. Antarctica's **glaciers** hold about three-

20   fourths of all the fresh water on Earth. Icebergs break off from the ice shelves. Some are larger than the big island of Hawaii. The winds are very strong. They are called the *katabatics*. These heavy winds blow up to 200 miles per hour. The **windchill factor** is very low. Diane Di Massa

longitude
imaginary vertical lines on the Earth used for navigation and telling time

glaciers
huge areas of ice flowing over land

windchill factor
the temperature of windless air that would have the same effect on exposed skin as a given combination of wind speed and air temperature

25 is an oceanographic engineer. She says, "This makes it
difficult and dangerous to do research here."

Even with the harsh weather, plants and animals can
survive in Antarctica. It is home to some very small life-
forms. Algae live along the coastlines. They live inside sea
30 ice. They survive in salty brine channels during the dark
winter. In springtime, when sea ice melts, they flow into
the ocean. These cells need sunlight and **carbon dioxide**
to grow. This is the basis of an important food chain. Next
on the food chain are krill. Krill look like small red shrimp.
35 They are a favorite food of Earth's largest mammal, the
endangered blue whale. Blue whales migrate to the southern
oceans to eat this rich food. Other animals visit Antarctica,
too. They include penguins, seabirds, seals, and other types
of whales.

40 Each summer, about 4,000 scientists from many
nations visit Antarctica. They go to do research. Some
people live on ships called icebreakers. Some live at land-
based research stations. Their supplies and food must all
be shipped or flown in. The scientists work hard to make
45 sure that human visitors do not pollute this fragile place.

Since 1976, the Antarctic Search for **Meteorites**
program has been at work. The program is searching for
clues about how and when our solar system formed. Scott
Sandford has been a team member on three field trips.
50 "I've probably found over 300 meteorites. I get excited
every time," he says. "One of our team's most surprising
discoveries was a
meteorite that was a piece
of Mars. Another was a
55 piece of the moon." One

carbon dioxide
a gas produced
during breakdown
of living matter

meteorites
parts of stone
or metal from a
meteor that have
landed on Earth

*Researchers in Antarctica
sometimes live on ships
called icebreakers.*

This meteorite, found on Antarctica, is about the size and weight of a car engine.

referred

known as

Leaf fossil found on Antarctica.

reason so many meteorites can be found on Antarctica is that the background is white or blue ice. The uneven shape and dark, glossy surface of a meteorite stand out.

60 Scientists have found fossils in Antarctica. There are fossils from dinosaurs and plants. Millions of years ago, Antarctica was not covered with glaciers. Plants and trees grew in a warm rain forest. At that time, the southern continents were one landmass. Scientists called it Gondwanaland. This and another landmass (Laurasia)

65 once made up a super-landmass. It's **referred** to as Pangea.

Antarctica is no longer connected with other continents. However, we are all linked by fragile ocean systems, the atmosphere, and a special place in the

70 universe. Humans have explored the Earth for thousands of years. We still have many mysteries to solve.

Adapted from "Mysteries of Antarctica" by Karen E. Lewis

Answer It
Say each answer in a complete sentence.

1. Explain why Antarctica is considered a mysterious continent.

2. Distinguish between the seasons in Antarctica and your hometown.

3. Categorize the jobs of a scientist working in Antarctica.

4. Explain why scientists search for meteorites in Antarctica.

5. Was Antarctica ever connected to other continents? Explain. Is it connected now? Explain.

THE FIRST TRANSCONTINENTAL RAILROAD

Time: Just past noon, May 10, 1869.

Place: Promontory, a tiny town on the shore of the Great Salt Lake in Utah.

Event: A large crowd gathers to witness a very important
5 ceremony. Telegraph wires wait to carry the news across the nation. Two locomotives idle on their tracks, nose to nose. One comes from the east, the other from the west. Six Irish men lay down the last rail from the east. Six Chinese men lay down the last rail from the west.

10   The president of the first transcontinental railroad gets ready. His job is to hammer in the last spike, to finally connect East and West. He swings and misses. The vice president of the Union Pacific Railroad misses, too! But the crowd cheers anyway. Other important
15 people take their turns. They hammer spikes of silver, iron, and gold into place. The first transcontinental railroad is complete!

Great Salt Lake
the shallow body of saltwater in northwestern Utah

transcontinental
spanning or crossing a continent

A Transcontinental Railroad

     Large groups of people were settling in California and the western territories. A group of businessmen predicted
20 that a railroad connecting the East and West Coasts would be a good idea. It could earn money in trade. They even talked about transporting goods brought to California from China.

     At first, it seemed impossible. But the Central Pacific
25 Railroad began construction in Sacramento, California, in 1863. The Union Pacific began in Omaha, Nebraska,

in December of the same year. In less than four years, workers laid 1,776 miles of track across a wilderness.

Both companies had huge problems getting supplies.
30 The Central Pacific had to ship equipment from the Atlantic coast. The only way to do this was by water. They had to send it either across the **Isthmus** of Panama or around **Cape** Horn to San Francisco. This was very expensive and took a long time.

35 The Union Pacific had its own problems. At first, it shipped supplies and equipment up the Missouri River by steamboat and then carried them overland by stagecoach and in wagons. Later, supplies went along tracks already laid. But this was slow. It took the labor of thousands to
40 complete this incredible transcontinental task.

isthmus

a narrow strip of land connecting two larger landmasses

cape

a point of land jutting into a body of water

Who Built the Transcontinental Railroad?

From the East: The Workers of the Union Pacific Railroad

One group of workers was employed by the Union Pacific Railroad. This railroad company had already reached Omaha. Now, it was moving west across the continent. It had all the workers it could use. Twelve
45 thousand men had drifted there from the North and the South. The Civil War was over. Privates, sergeants, lieutenants, captains, and colonels were unemployed. Soldiers from both sides needed work. Former slaves needed work. Ex-convicts needed work. The biggest
50 group was the Irish. Many of them had fought in the war. Many others were fresh off the boat from Ireland.

Living conditions were difficult. The men lived in tents or in converted boxcars. Towns sprang up at the end of the line. These towns were portable. After about
55 50 miles of new track had been laid, the merchants and townspeople raced up the track to set up a new town. They took down their **flimsy** buildings, which often had canvas roofs. They piled everything on wagons and set up again at the new spot.

flimsy

without strength or stability

From the West: The Workers of the Central Pacific Railroad

60   Another group of workers was employed by the Central Pacific Railroad. This company was laying track from Sacramento, California. It would join the Union Pacific Railroad, which was
65 crawling out from Omaha. The railroad bosses of the Central Pacific Railroad had a more difficult time finding reliable workers. Many would quit after a week or two. They worked only long enough to earn money.
70 Then, they would go back to prospecting for gold.

Thousands labored to complete the Transcontinental Railroad.

    In 1849, the Chinese came to California for gold. Immigration from China had brought many Chinese to the western United States. Many went to work for the railroad. They were smaller in stature. But everyone
75 learned that their smaller size didn't matter. The Chinese roadbed was straighter, smoother, and longer than that of any other crew. The Chinese worked without stopping. Their cooks would walk among them with steaming buckets of tea, hung from long rods across their
80 shoulders. That was enough to get them through the day.

    The Chinese railroad workers became known for their courage. Once, a railroad bed was needed halfway up a **precipice** overlooking the American River gorge. Construction seemed impossible. The Chinese offered to
85 try. They asked for reeds. They wove waist-high baskets with eyelets for inserting ropes. These baskets, with one or two men in each, were lowered halfway down the cliff. Then the men used tiny hand drills and inserted blasting powder into the side of the cliff. The resulting blast

precipice

an extremely steep or overhanging place

90 created a surface on which the track could be built. The workers were quickly pulled to safety before the explosion, but not always fast enough. Because of the bravery of these men, the railroad bed was built.

When the railroads met at Promontory, Utah, on 95 May 10, 1869, a photograph was taken. Not one of the 13,000 Chinese workers was in it. Had the western railroad been built by invisible men? The Central Pacific could not have laid its railroad without the Chinese. Chinese workers' bones are buried on either 100 side of the tracks. The railroad itself is a memorial to them.

Adapted from "The Builders of the First Transcontinental Railroad" by Charlotte Gemmell

The reconstructed trains, named 119 and Jupiter, met in Promontory, Utah, at the Golden Spike Ceremony on May 10, 1994.

Answer It
Say each answer in a complete sentence.

1. Distinguish between the different transportation problems encountered by both railroad companies.

2. Compare the Union Pacific Railroad workers and the Central Pacific Railroad workers.

3. Describe the living conditions for the railroad workers.

4. Why do you think the Chinese workers were left out of the photograph taken at the completion of the railroad?

5. Compare the mood conveyed by the author in the first two paragraphs with the mood in the last paragraph.

Continental Drift

People living high in the mountains of Nepal and the **plateaus** of Tibet collect seashells even though many have never seen a beach or the sea. Off in the distance **looms** Mount Everest, the highest mountain in the
5 world. Its snow-covered peaks reveal layer upon layer of ocean-deposited sands, now hardened into rock. The Indian Ocean lies many miles to the southeast, 26,000 feet lower.

    Some of the people must wonder how the shells
10 got there. Were ancient sea levels much higher? Did floodwater carry the shells there? Were the mountains very much lower?

What Stories Can the Seashells Tell Us?

    The story that the shells and fossils of the Himalayan Mountains tell is a very old one. It starts more than 105
15 million years ago. This is the age that scientists give to the shells and the rocks in which they are preserved. It tells of a vast warm ocean separating Europe and Asia from an independent continent of India. That ocean, called the Tethys Sea, was home to a wide variety of
20 creatures. For millions of years, layers of shells were preserved. They lay in the sands that settled to the bottom of the sea's shallow, quiet waters.

plateaus
elevated, level areas of land

looms
appears as a very large shape

Crashing Continents

Then, just as now, the stiff outer crust of Earth was broken into many jigsaw pieces. These pieces are called
25 tectonic plates. Tectonic plates are giant sheets of solid rock near the Earth's surface. They slide along the top of a hotter, more liquid layer. The plates act like giant conveyor belts. They constantly shift the positions of the continents on the Earth's surface. When the animals
30 in the seashells were alive, the land that is now called India was pushing northward. It moved on its own plate at the great speed of about 36 feet per century. As India approached, most of the oceanic bottom between the continents was forced downward into Earth's **mantle**.
35 But some small fragments were swept up against Asia. These fragments contained the fossil shells. Finally, about 40 to 50 million years ago, India rammed into the landmass of Europe and Asia! The continents **fused** together, forming a very thick continental crust. But
40 *still* the plate was forcing India northward. The land crumpled under the **immense** pressure and was folded and lifted. Mountains formed. Today, the Himalayan Mountains and the Tibetan plateau are still rising, as India continues to squeeze against its northern neighbor.

mantle

a layer of the Earth between the crust and the core

fused

combined, became united

immense

extremely large, huge

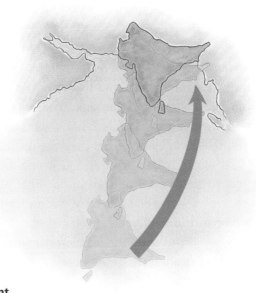

India crashes into Asia in slow motion.

45 The movement isn't as rapid now, but the Himalayas, the highest mountains in the world, rise ⅕ inch higher each year. And so do those ancient seashells!

The Pangea Puzzle

Modern scientists believe that once the continents were one landmass. In 1912, the German scientist Alfred
50 Wegener first proposed that the continents started as one huge landmass that had drifted apart. Most people thought he was crazy.

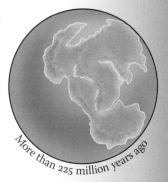

More than 225 million years ago

Wegener was the first scientist to publish a scientific paper stating that the world originally had only one
55 continent. He wasn't the first person to think this. But he was the first one brave enough to announce it to the world. Several people had noticed that the continents could fit together like pieces of a jigsaw puzzle. This was especially noticeable with the west coast of Africa and the
60 east coast of South America. Remove the 4,000 miles of ocean that lay between them. They fit together perfectly. Other things, too, pointed to the fact that they had once been joined.

About 150 million years ago

Mountain ridges on one continent could be matched
65 to mountain ridges on the other. The mountains had the same structure and the same type of rocks. When you fitted the two continents together, the ends of the mountain ranges lined up.

Scientists also knew that fossils belonging to the
70 same animals and plants could be found on different continents, separated by thousands of miles of ocean.

Today

Wegener also noticed that fossils found in some areas could not possibly have survived the climatic conditions there. For instance, some fossils found on Antarctica
75 could never have survived the cold conditions there. Those animals and plants must have originally been much nearer to the **equator** .

Wegener proposed a theory. He said that more than 225 million years ago, there was just one enormous
80 "supercontinent." He called it Pangea. It consisted of all Earth's landmasses locked together. Then, he said,

equator

an imaginary line dividing Earth's northern and southern hemispheres something caused it to split apart. The parts drifted through the oceans, until they reached the places they are now.

85   Scientists believe that plate tectonics cause continents of solid rock to change positions. Some continents move farther apart and some closer together. Our continents, carried by these giant stone rafts, crawl across the surface of the planet. They inch along at about the same
90 rate your fingernails grow. Who knows? Plate tectonics may produce another mountain range as high as the Himalayas. Maybe there will be another Pangea—225 million years from now.

Adapted from "Seashells on the Summit," by Gretchen Noyes-Hull, and "The Pangea Puzzle," by Mary Reina

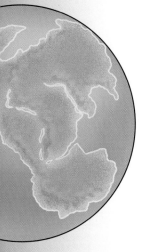

Pangea consisted of all Earth's landmasses locked together.

Think About It

1. People who live atop the mountains of Nepal and the plateaus of Tibet collect seashells. Select possible explanations for the shells' presence.

2. The author writes that the shells and fossils found atop the Himalayas tell a story. Explain why this statement is an example of *personification* (a literary device).

3. Distinguish between Alfred Wegener's theory and the theories of those who thought differently.

4. List the ideas that seem to support Wegener's theory.

5. Discuss the possible reasons why Alfred Wegener had the courage to announce his theory to the world. Discuss other ideas that may take courage to share with others.

6. Use a globe or a map to locate the following: Mount Everest, the Himalayan Mountains, and the Indian Ocean. Distinguish these locations from where you live.

The Quest for a Continent

Rodrigo de Triana, lookout
on a small square-rigged sailing
ship named the Pinta, shouted,
"Tierra!" It was shortly after
5 midnight in October 1492, and
these were welcome words.
The boom of a cannon signaled
the sighting to the Pinta's two
companion ships. The three
10 vessels lowered their sails to
wait for daylight; then, they
would investigate the landfall.
They had been sailing in search
of land since early August.
15   The ships were Spanish,
and they sailed under Captain General Cristóbal Colón.
Historical evidence does not tell us much about this man
or his journey. Colón called himself by different names
during his lifetime; he was called Cristoforo Colombo,
20 Christobal Colom, and Xpoual de Colón (his signature
in the journal he kept during his 1492 voyage). Today we
remember him as Christopher Columbus.
    Columbus was a sailor most of his life. He
made many voyages on merchant ships, first in the
25 **Mediterranean**, and later along the Atlantic coasts of
Europe and northern Africa. He also worked for a while
as a cartographer (maker of maps and sailing charts) in
Lisbon, Portugal. He read books that told of the journeys
of Marco Polo and other explorers, books that revealed

*The flagship of
Columbus' 1492
voyage—the
Santa Maria.*

Mediterranean
the inland sea
surrounded by
Europe, Africa,
and Asia

Queen Isabella.

30 what was known about the lands and seas of the world at that time. In 1479, he married Felipa Moniz Perestrella, and within a year or so, they had a son they 35 named Diego.

Perhaps geography books inspired him. We don't know for sure. But we do know that Columbus approached the king of 40 Portugal in 1484 with an idea. He wished to sail in search of "islands and mainlands in the Ocean Sea." He needed an investor to back what he called "the Enterprise of the Indies." The king's advisers rejected his request for ships and money.

45 Columbus' wife had died, so he took Diego and traveled to Spain to try his luck there. In 1486, he obtained an **audience** with Queen Isabella. She was intrigued, but her advisers were not convinced of the **feasibility** of Columbus' plan. She asked him to wait. In 50 1490, the queen turned down his proposal, but Columbus kept waiting and trying. Finally, early in 1492, Isabella agreed to **finance** the plan.

Captain General Columbus was about 40 years old when his ships left the small Spanish port of Palos. 55 Perhaps as a result of the books he had read and the sailors he had met, he was convinced that the western shores of Asia, called the Indies (for India), could be reached by sailing west. Until then, the **profitable** trade with these foreign lands had gone east, a long and 60 difficult journey.

Little evidence confirms that Asia was his goal. It may be that Columbus wanted an opportunity to search for fabled islands that sailors spoke of or other lands of great importance. Columbus sailed with a command 65 from Isabella to "discover and **acquire** . . . islands and mainlands in the Ocean Sea," and to call himself "Viceroy and Governor-General" of the lands he discovered.

audience
a formal meeting with a high-ranking person (e.g., queen or Pope)

feasibility
the likelihood of being accomplished

finance
to pay for

profitable
producing benefits such as money

acquire
to gain possession of, to obtain

Whatever he considered his destination, Columbus knew that if he succeeded, he would achieve glory. During his lifetime, trade with foreign lands was growing, so discovery of new lands and markets brought wealth and fame to those who claimed them. They had no idea that two huge, unrecorded continents—North and South America—lay to the west.

So his journey began. After weeks of sailing on the open sea, struggling to encourage his nervous crew and quiet their fears that they would never see land again, Columbus recorded in his journal signs of land—floating branches and flocks of birds. The next morning, Rodrigo de Triana saw the moon shining on the cliffs and sandy beach of an island.

In truth, Columbus did not know exactly where he was, except in terms of the time he had traveled west from the Canary Islands off the African continent. He called his landfall "the Indies" because he believed he had reached the Asian continent. Actually, several years passed before navigators realized that he had reached a group of islands off the coast of two unrecorded continents.

Columbus was called a discoverer of new lands, but he was not the first to discover them. The islands and continents he found were already inhabited by millions of people. Many of them had societies as advanced as those in Europe. He was not even the first European to reach these

Columbus on the deck of the Santa Maria, *watching for land.*

105 lands. But he was the first to return there more than
once.

Even though he was not the first European to
discover the existence of the new continents, Columbus
is historically important. He began a process of change,
110 both for the people in these "new" lands and for the
people who lived on other continents. Why was that
important? For the first time, people of all continents
were aware of each other and of the numbers of
continents in their world.

Adapted from "A Stranger to Foreign Shores" by Beth Weston

Think About It

1. What can you infer Rodrigo de Triana meant when he
   shouted, "Tierra!"?

2. Summarize the struggle Columbus endured to find
   an investor for his quest.

3. Explain why Columbus' voyage was such an
   important historical event.

4. Compare and contrast the voyages of today's
   astronauts and cosmonauts with the voyages of
   Christopher Columbus.

5. It was very common for sailors to be at sea for
   months at a time. What do you think was difficult
   about spending so much time away from land?

6. Columbus was called a discoverer of new lands, yet
   these lands had been inhabited for many years. If
   you were one of the inhabitants, how would you
   feel knowing Columbus received all the credit for
   discovering your land? Why?

English Consonant Chart

(Note the voiceless/voiced consonant phoneme pairs)

Mouth Position

Type of Consonant Sound	Bilabial (lips)	Labiodental (lips/teeth)	Dental (tongue between teeth)	Alveolar (tongue behind teeth)	Palatal (roof of mouth)	Velar (back of mouth)	Glottal (throat)
Stops	/p/ /b/			/t/ /d/		/k/ /g/	
Fricatives		/f/ /v/	/th/ /t͟h/	/s/ /z/	/sh/ /zh/		/h/[1]
Affricatives					/ch/ /j/		
Nasals	/m/			/n/		/ng/	
Lateral				/l/			
Semivowels	/ʰw/ /w/[2]			/r/	/y/		

1   Classed as a fricative on the basis of acoustic effect. It is like a vowel without voice.

2   /ʰw/ and /w/ are velar as well as bilabial, as the back of the tongue is raised as it is for /u/.

Adapted with permission from Bolinger, D. 1975. *Aspects of Language* (2nd ed.). Harcourt Brace Jovanovich, p. 41.

English Vowel Chart

ē		**ĭ**
1. me		1. sit
2. these		2. gym
3. see		
4. eat		
5. chief		
6. happy		
7. key		
8. either		

ā
1. baby
2. make
3. rain
4. play
5. eight
6. vein
7. they
8. great
9. straight

ĕ
1. pet
2. head

ə
1. about
2. lesson
3. elect
4. definition
5. circus

ă
1. cat

ī
1. item
2. time
3. pie
4. my
5. right

ŏ
1. fox
2. swap

ŭ
1. cup
2. cover
3. flood
4. tough
5. among

aw
1. saw
2. pause
3. call
4. dog
5. wall

ō
1. go
2. vote
3. boat
4. show
5. toe

o͝o
1. took
2. put
3. could

o͞o
1. moo
2. ruby
3. tube
4. chew
5. blue
6. suit
7. soup

er
her
fur
sir

ar
cart

or
sport

oi	**oy**
oil	boy

ou	**ow**
out	cow

Note: The order of spelling examples reflects the relative frequency of incidence for that spelling of the phoneme.

Vowel Chart based on Moats, L.C. (2003). *LETRS: Language Essentials for Teachers of Reading and Spelling*, Module 2 (p. 98). Adapted with permission of the author. All rights reserved. Published by Sopris West Educational Services.

Language! Pronunciation Key

Consonants

p	**p**u**p**, ra**pp**ed, **p**ie	zh	vi**s**ion, trea**s**ure, a**z**ure
b	**b**o**b**, e**bb**, **b**rother	h	**h**at, **h**ere, **h**ope
t	**t**ire, jump**ed**, hur**t**	ch	**ch**ur**ch**, ma**tch**, bea**ch**
d	**d**ee**d**, ma**d**, file**d**	j	**j**u**dg**e, en**j**oy, **j**ell
k	**c**at, **k**i**ck**, **c**ut	m	**m**op
g	**g**et, **g**ill, ma**g**azine	n	**n**ot
f	**f**lu**ff**, rou**gh**, **ph**oto	ng	si**ng**
v	**v**al**v**e, e**v**ery, ele**v**en	l	**l**and
th	**th**in, **th**ree, ma**th**		
<u>th</u>	**th**is, **th**ere, mo**th**er	w	**w**ith, **w**agon, **w**est
s	**s**od, **c**ity, li**s**t	r	**r**amp
z	**z**ebra, ha**s**, bee**s**	y	**y**ard, **y**es, **y**ellow
sh	**sh**ip, **s**ugar, ma**ch**ine		

Vowels

ē	b**ee**t	(bēt)	ō	b**oa**t	(bōt)
ĭ	b**i**t	(bĭt)	o͝o	p**u**t	(po͝ot)
ā	b**ai**t	(bāt)	o͞o	b**oo**t	(bo͞ot)
ĕ	b**e**t	(bĕt)	oi	b**oi**l	(boil)
ă	b**a**t	(băt)	ou	p**ou**t	(pout)
ī	b**i**te	(bīt)	î	p**eer**	(pîr)
ŏ	p**o**t	(pŏt)	â	b**ear**	(bâr)
ô	b**ou**ght	(bôt)	ä	p**ar**	(pär)
ŭ	b**u**t	(bŭt)	ô	b**ore**	(bôr)
ə	rabb**i**t	(ră' bət)	û	p**ear**l	(pûrl)

a	art	beside	camshaft	collect
above	aspect	better	candidate	color
acorn	assess	bird	candy	combat
across	assist	birth	canine	comma
adapt	athlete	blacktop	cannon	command
addend	atlas	blanket	canter	commend
addict	attach	blemish	canyon	commit
adding	awake	blockade	car	common
admire	awhile	blossom	cargo	compact
adult	baby	body	carpet	compile
advertise	backbone	bonnet	cart	complete
affect	badly	border	cartel	complex
after	ballot	bore	carve	compose
again	banjo	born	cascade	compress
ago	bankrupt	bottom	casket	comprise
album	bar	briskly	catnap	compute
alive	bark	broken	certain	concave
alone	barn	bronco	channel	concrete
along	baseline	brother	chapter	conduct
altitude	basic	bucket	charm	confess
amend	basin	buddy	chart	conflict
anger	basket	buggy	charter	congress
angry	be	bullet	checklist	connect
another	became	bumpy	chicken	conquer
answer	become	bunny	children	conquest
antilock	bedside	burn	china	consent
antitheft	before	burning	church	consist
antitoxin	beforehand	burst	clamshell	constant
append	began	butter	classmate	constrict
apron	begin	button	clerk	construct
archway	beginner	by	climate	consult
are	begun	bypass	clockwork	contact
arm	behave	cabstand	closet	contempt
army	being	cactus	clover	content
arrive	belly	campfire	cluster	contest
arrived	belong	campus	collar	continent

contract	define	discuss	eclipse	evil
contrast	delete	disfavor	educate	evolve
convent	deliver	disgust	ego	exactly
convert	demote	disinfect	Egypt	exclude
convict	denim	dismiss	elastic	exempt
copy	density	dispel	elect	exhale
cord	dentist	dispose	electric	exile
core	deny	dispute	elope	expand
corn	depart	disregard	embargo	expend
corner	depress	disrespect	empire	expert
correct	derby	disrupt	empty	explode
cotton	derive	dissect	engine	explore
cover	describe	distinct	enlist	explorer
covered	desert	distort	enrich	exploring
craftsmen	deserve	distrust	enter	export
crater	despite	disturb	entered	expose
crazy	detect	disturbingly	enterprise	extend
create	detector	diverse	entire	extent
cricket	devote	divert	entrap	extract
cried	diameter	divided	entry	extreme
crisis	dictate	divine	entryway	eye
cry	dictator	dockyard	envy	factor
crypt	dictatorship	doctor	enzyme	factors
crystal	diet	dolly	episode	fantastic
cubic	differ	dominate	equal	far
curly	difficulty	dozen	equate	farm
current	diffuse	dragon	equator	farmer
daddy	dignity	driver	equip	farmers
dark	dilate	driveway	erase	farmland
darling	dilute	dropkick	erode	farther
data	dioxide	droplet	erupt	favor
day	direct	dry	escape	feline
debate	dirt	dryly	estate	fern
decade	discard	during	evade	fever
decline	discover	dusty	evaluate	fiber
decode	discovered	duty	even	fifty
defend	discredit	dye	event	figure
defense	discrete	dynamic	ever	final

finger
fingers
finish
finished
finite
fir
firefly
firm
first
fishnet
flavor
flu
fly
flyer
focus
for
forest
forget
forgive
forgot
fork
form
former
forty
fossil
framework
franchise
frankly
freshly
fro
frosty
fry
fuel
funny
fur
further
furthermore
gabby

gallon
gallop
gangway
garden
gases
gasket
gateway
girl
girth
gladly
glory
glossy
go
gone
good
govern
granny
grapevine
gravel
gravity
great
grimly
grizzly
halo
hamburger
hamlet
hammer
handshake
handy
happen
happened
happily
happy
harbor
hard
hardy
harsh
harvest

hasty
hatchway
hello
helmet
her
herd
hereby
hero
hi
hi fi
hillside
hobby
holly
homeland
homemade
homesick
homework
horn
horse
horseback
hotel
human
hundred
hunger
hungry
hurricane
hurriedly
hurry
hurt
husband
hybrid
I
idea
imply
impose
incline
include
indent

indigo
indirect
infant
infect
infer
inflate
inflect
inflict
inhabit
inhale
inject
injure
inland
input
inrush
insane
insect
insects
inset
inside
inspect
instep
instinct
instruct
insult
intact
intend
intense
intent
interact
intercom
interest
interesting
interject
interlock
Internet
interpret
interrupt

intersect
intervene
invade
invent
invest
invite
invoke
involve
iris
item
ivy
jacket
jar
jelly
jellyfish
jolly
judo
jumbo
jury
kimono
kitten
labor
ladder
lady
lantern
laptop
lasso
lately
later
laugh
lazily
lazy
leftover
legal
lemon
letter
levy
liar

liberty	member	myself	oil	passive
lifelike	members	myth	omit	pastry
lifeline	membership	namesake	oneself	pasture
lifetime	memo	nasty	ongoing	pathway
likewise	menu	navy	only	pattern
lily	merchants	negate	open	pavement
limestone	meter	nerve	oppose	pecan
limit	method	never	or	pelvis
linen	migrant	nevermore	orbit	penny
linked	migrate	new	order	pensive
lion	military	nickel	organ	people
little	minister	ninety	organic	pepper
lively	minor	nitrate	other	per
livestock	minute	no	otherwise	perfect
local	minutes	nobility	over	perfume
locate	missive	nobody	overcast	perhaps
located	mistake	nonfat	overcome	permissive
locket	misty	nonsense	overdose	permit
locust	modem	nonskid	overhang	person
lofty	modern	nonstop	overlap	pigpen
look	moment	nor	overrun	pilgrim
lucky	monster	normal	overtake	pilot
lumber	monthly	north	overtime	planet
madly	more	northern	oxide	planets
magnet	moreover	number	ozone	plaster
magnetic	morning	nurse	palate	platform
major	mortar	nylon	pallet	plenty
mandate	most	oasis	pancake	plural
march	motel	obese	panel	pocket
maritime	mother	object	pantry	poem
mark	motive	observe	paper	polite
market	motor	observer	paperback	pollute
matchbox	motto	obstruct	parade	polo
matter	multitude	obtuse	park	polygon
may	mummy	occur	parkway	pony
me	murder	oddly	part	poor
medic	music	offense	partner	popcorn
melon	my	offer	party	poppy

porch	protest	repetitive	sadly	sly
pore	provide	reply	safety	smart
port	pupil	report	salad	so
positive	puppy	reporter	salesman	softly
poster	purchase	represent	sandpaper	solely
poverty	purpose	reprint	sandstone	solo
predicate	purse	republic	sandy	somebody
predict	pyramid	request	sanitary	sore
prefab	quantity	require	satisfy	sorry
prefix	quickly	rerun	say	sort
prehistoric	quiet	reserve	score	sound
premise	radish	reserves	second	spark
present	random	resolve	secret	spider
preset	ransom	respect	secrets	splendid
preshrunk	rarely	respond	secure	sport
presume	rascal	restore	see	spotted
pretend	rather	restrict	select	spy
prettily	react	result	serve	squirrel
pretty	reborn	return	server	stalemate
prevent	recall	revamp	seven	stampede
primary	record	reverse	shark	star
primitive	recover	revise	sharp	starch
printer	redo	revive	she	start
prior	refer	reword	shipped	starve
priority	refine	ribbon	shirt	statement
prison	reflect	richly	shore	status
private	reform	right	shoreline	stiffly
pro	refund	riot	short	store
problem	regard	river	shortly	storm
products	reject	robot	shy	stormy
program	relapse	rocket	silent	story
prohibit	relax	rodent	silly	storyteller
project	rely	rodeo	silver	strengthen
promise	remember	rubber	simply	stressful
promote	remorse	ruin	sir	strictly
promptly	remote	rural	sister	strongly
property	remote	rusty	sixty	student
protect	reorder	rye	sky	students

study	symbols	total	underline	verse
style	symptom	traffic	underpass	veto
subject	syntax	transact	undershirt	vibrate
submit	synthetic	transcribe	undersized	video
subset	syrup	transfer	understand	vindictive
subtotal	system	transitive	understandingly	vinyl
subtract	tablet	translate	underwater	visit
suburb	tadpole	transmit	undress	volcano
sudden	taffy	transplant	unfit	volume
suddenly	target	transport	unhand	wagon
summer	template	trapped	unify	want
sunny	tempo	tribute	unit	water
sunrise	tender	tried	unite	way
sunshine	term	trigger	unlike	we
super	termite	trombone	unlock	western
superego	thesis	try	unmask	whatever
superhero	thickly	turbine	unpack	whether
superman	thinning	turn	unplug	why
supermarket	third	twenty	unrest	windpipe
superscript	thirty	type	unwell	windy
supersonic	though	ugly	unwise	winter
superstar	through	umpire	uppercase	woman
supplies	thunder	unbend	upset	wonder
supply	ticket	unbent	urban	work
suppose	tiger	unclad	useless	yard
surprise	tiny	unclasp	valuate	yarn
survive	tiresome	under	vanish	year
suspect	today	underarm	varsity	zero
suspend	tomorrow	underbrush	vastly	
swiftly	tornado	undercut	velvet	
symbol	torpedo	undergo	verb	

The definitions that accompany the readings relate to the context of the readings. They are provided to help students understand the specific reading selection. For complete definitions of these words, consult a dictionary. Pronunciations are taken from the *American Heritage® Dictionary of the English Language*, Fourth Edition.

achieves (ə-chēvz')—completes successfully, accomplishes

acquire (ə-kwīr')—to gain possession of, to obtain

adapted (ə-dăp'tĭd)—used a skill in a new way

adhere (ăd-hîr')—to stick closely to

adjoining (ə-joi'nĭng)—next to, connecting

amateur (ăm'ə-tûr')—unpaid; plays for pleasure, not pay

annoyed (ə-noid')—irritated, upset

anxious (ăngk'shəs)—worried, nervous, or afraid

ascended (ə-sĕn'dĭd)—rose from a lower level or station; advanced

audience (ô'dē-əns)—a formal meeting with a high-ranking person (e.g., queen or Pope)

boundary (boun'də-rē)—an edge or border that marks a specific area

Britain (brĭt'n)—a western European island nation, comprising England, Scotland, Wales, and Northern Ireland

cape (kāp)—a point of land jutting into a body of water

carbon dioxide (kär'bən dī-ŏk'sīd)—a gas produced during the breakdown of living matter

cargo (kär'gō)—products carried by ship, plane, or another vehicle

catapults (kăt'ə-pŭlts')—machines used by soldiers to shoot big rocks against the enemy

ceased (sēst)—stopped

charitable (chăr'ĭ-tə-bəl)—generous; giving help or money to those who need it

choreographer (kôr'ē-ŏg'rəf-ər)—a person who plans and directs a dance performance

clever (klĕv'ər)—very smart, good at solving problems

competitor (kəm-pĕt'ĭ-tər)—a person who participates in a sport

considerable (kən-sĭd'ər-ə-bəl)—large in size or amount

contents (kŏn'tĕnts')—something contained

controversial (kŏn'trə-vûr'shəl)—causing arguments or disagreements

conveying (kən-vā'ĭng)—carrying

cosmonauts (kŏz'mə-nôts')—Russian astronauts

deactivated (dē-ăk'tə-vā'tĭd)—stopped something from working

deciphering (dĭ-sī'fər-ĭng)—changing a secret code into known words

decoding (dē-kō'dĭng)—reading secret codes

defunct (dĭ-fŭngkt')—no longer in existence or working

dejectedly (dĭ-jĕk'tĭd-lē)—in a low-spirited or depressed way

descendants (dĭ-sĕn'dənts)—children and relatives of one family

diagnosis (dī'əg-nō'sĭs)—the nature of an illness or injury determined by a doctor who has examined signs and symptoms

dilemma (dĭ-lĕm'ə)—a problem that doesn't seem to have a solution

documents (dŏk'yə-mənts)—papers that give information or proof of something

drastically (drăs'tĭk-lē)—suddenly, severely

Egyptologists (ē'jĭp-tŏl'ə-jĭsts)—people who study ancient Egypt, including its history, culture, and artifacts

enabled (ĕ-nā'bəld)—made possible

encased (ĕn-kāst')—completely closed or wrapped in

encoding (ĕn-kōd'ĭng)—writing in secret codes

endorsement (ĕn-dôrs'mənt)—a legal document allowing companies to use your name for profit

equator (ĭ-kwā'tər)—an imaginary line dividing Earth's northern and southern hemispheres

evidence (ĕv'ĭ-dəns)—information or things that show proof

facet (făs'ĭt)—one part

feasibility (fē'zə-bĭl'ĭ-tē)—the likelihood of being accomplished

feasible (fē'zə-bəl)—possible

finance (fə-năns')—to pay for

financial (fə-năn'shəl)—related to money

flammable (flăm'ə-bəl)—able to catch on fire easily

flimsy (flĭm'zē)—without strength or stability

focused (fō'kəst)—kept attention on a goal without distraction

fortifications (fôr'tə-fĭ-kā'shənz)—walls or structures used to protect soldiers

fused (fyo͞ozd)—combined, became united

galactic (gə-lăk'tĭk)—star-like

genius (jēn'yəs)—an outstanding ability

gesture (jĕs'chər)—an action meant to show feeling or that is done for effect

gilded (gĭl'dĭd)—covered or coated with gold

glaciers (glā'shərs)—huge areas of ice flowing over land

gratitude (grăt'ĭ-to͞od')—thankfulness; appreciation

Great Salt Lake (grāt sôlt lāk)—the shallow body of saltwater in northwestern Utah

helium (hē'lē-əm)—colorless, odorless gas that weighs less than air

immense (ĭ-mĕns')—extremely large, huge

immersed (ĭ-mûrst')—became completely involved in something

impenetrable (ĭm-pĕn'ĭ-trə-bəl)—incapable of being passed through

imported (ĭm-pôr'tĭd)—brought in from another country

indispensable (ĭn'dĭ-spĕn'sə-bəl)—absolutely necessary

inspiration (ĭn'spə-rā'shən)—motivation to take action

intercepting (ĭn'tər-sĕp'tĭng)—interrupting or stopping the movement or progress of something

international (ĭn'tər-năsh'ə-nəl)—of two or more nations

intertwined (ĭn'tər-twīnd')—twisted, wound around

intervals (ĭn'tər-vəlz)—spaces between objects or measured points

invested (ĭn-vĕs'tĭd)—put time, effort, or money into something

invincible (ĭn-vĭn'sə-bəl)—too strong to be defeated

invulnerable (ĭn-vŭl'nər-ə-bəl)—not able to be hurt

isthmus (ĭs'məs)—a narrow strip of land connecting two larger landmasses

jettisoning (jĕt'ĭ-sə-nĭng)—throwing, sending off

Kevlar (kĕv'lär)—a name used for a special type of fiber

legacy (lĕg'ə-sē)—anything that is passed down from ancestors or someone who came before

limestone (līm'stōn')—a kind of rock formed mostly from shells and other animal remains

local (lō'kəl)—having to do with a particular place, such as a neighborhood or a town

longitude (lŏn'jĭ-tōōd')—imaginary vertical lines on the Earth used for navigation and telling time

looms (lōōmz)—appears as a very large shape

lurks (lûrks)—waits, hides in waiting

makeshift (māk'shĭft')—temporary substitute for something else

mantle (măn'tl)—a layer of the Earth between the crust and the core

marrow (măr'ō)—the soft tissue that fills the hollow centers of most bones

marshes (mär'shĭz)—low, wet areas, often thick with tall grasses; bogs

Mediterranean (mĕd'ĭ-tə-rā'nē-ən)—the inland sea surrounded by Europe, Africa, and Asia

meteorites (mē'tē-ə-rīts')—parts of stone or metal from a meteor that have landed on Earth

miniature (mĭn'ē-ə-chŏŏr')—a very small model of something

mocking (mŏk'ĭng)—making fun of by imitating

moody (mōō'dē)—angry or sad

motion (mō'shən)—movement

motto (mŏt'ō)—a short saying that states a basic belief or goal

Nile River (nīl rĭv'ər)—the longest river in the world, running through nine African countries and emptying into the Mediterranean Sea

nobleman (nō'bəl-mən)—a man of high rank or title

orientation (ôr'ē-ĕn-tā'shən)—location or position

palace (păl'ĭs)—the official home of a king or queen or other persons of high rank or authority

patented (păt'n-tĭd)—obtained the right to make, use, or sell an invention

peasant (pĕz'ənt)—a poor farmer

perfectionist (pər-fĕk'shə-nĭst)—a person who tries to do things without making any mistakes

perils (pĕr'əlz)—dangers, threats

persistence (pər-sĭs'təns)—trying hard without giving up

phoenix (fē'nĭks)—a mythological bird that lived for 500 years, set itself on fire, then was born again from its ashes

pigments (pĭg'mənts)—powders or pastes mixed with liquid to make colors

plateaus (plă-tōz')—elevated, level areas of land

pounce (pouns)—to attack by jumping or swooping down quickly

preceding (prĭ-sēd'ĭng)—coming before in time

precipice (prĕs'ə-pĭs)—extremely steep or overhanging place

precision (prĭ-sĭzh'ən)—the state of being accurate or exact

prehistoric (prē'hĭ-stôr'ĭk)—belonging to a period of time before written history

profitable (prŏf'ĭ-tə-bəl)—producing benefits such as money

prolific (prə-lĭf'ĭk)—very productive

promoting (prə-mōt'ĭng)—supporting, contributing to

prototype (prō'tə-tīp')—an original model used for testing before producing the final version

Puerto Rico (pwĕr'tə rē'kō)—a self-governing island of the U.S. in the Caribbean Sea

rare (râr)—not often found or seen

realm (rĕlm)—a royal kingdom

reconstruct (rē'kən-strŭkt')—to make over in the mind or as a function of memory

reference (rĕf'ər-əns)—a source of information

referred (rĭ-fûrd')—known as

relief (rĭ-lēf')—the feeling of being freed from pain

Renaissance (rĕn'ĭ-säns')—the revival of art, literature, and learning that began in Europe in the 14th century and lasted into the 17th century

revitalize (rē-vīt'l-īz')—to give new life or energy to something

rotisserie (rō-tĭs'ə-rē)—a cooking device that turns meat while it cooks

Sahara Desert (sə-hâr'ə dĕz'ərt)—a large North African desert

scholars (skŏl'ərz)—students

seals (sēlz)—designs or raised emblems showing something is official

sensor (sĕn'sər)—a device used for identifying something by heat, movement, light, or sound

skeptical (skĕp'tĭ-kəl)—doubtful, uncertain

solo (sō'lō)—alone

species (spē'shēz)—groups of similar animals

stance (stăns)—a body position of an athlete ready to take action

striving (strī'vĭng)—working very hard; trying

transcontinental (trăns'kŏn-tə-nĕn'tl)—spanning or crossing a continent

transfixed (trăns-fĭkst')—held still and staring at something without noticing anything else

translucent (trăns-lōō'sənt)—see-through, transparent

ultimate (ŭl'tə-mĭt)—greatest possible; highest

unconventional (ŭn'kən-vĕn'shə-nəl)—not ordinary, unusual

venture (vĕn'chər)—to do something that is dangerous or daring

villain (vĭl'ən)—bad person

virtually (vûr'chōo-ə-lē)—for the most part; practically

volunteers (vŏl'ən-tîrz')—people who perform a service for free

vulnerable (vŭl'nər-ə-bəl)—unprotected, open to harm

windchill factor (wĭnd'chĭl' făk'tər)—the temperature of windless air that would have the same effect on exposed skin as a given combination of wind speed and air temperature

wits (wĭts)—smart thinking in a difficult situation

Signal Words Based on Bloom's Taxonomy

Category	Meaning	Location
Remember Units 7–8	Retrieve relevant knowledge from long-term memory	
list	state a series of names, ideas, or events	Unit 7
locate	find specific information	
name	label specific information	
recognize	know something from prior experience or learning	
state	say or write specific information	
describe	state detailed information about an idea or concept	Unit 8
recall	retrieve information from memory to provide an answer	
repeat	say specific infomation again	
retrieve	locate information from memory to provide an answer	
Understand Units 9–12	Construct meaning from instructional messages, including oral, written, and graphic communication	
conclude	arrive at logical end based on specific information	Unit 9
define in your own words	tell the meaning of something in one's own words	
illustrate	present an example or explanation in pictures or words	
predict	foretell new information from what is already known	
tell	say or write specific information	
identify	locate specific information in the text	Unit 10
paraphrase	restate information in somewhat different words to simplify and clarify	
summarize	restate important ideas and details from multiple paragraphs or sources	

Category	Meaning	Location
categorize	place information into groups	Unit 11
classify	organize into groups with similar characteristics	
discuss	talk about or examine a subject with others	
match	put together things that are alike or similar	
sort	place or separate into groups	
compare	state the similarities between two or more ideas	Unit 12
contrast	state the differences between two or more ideas	
explain	express understanding of an idea or concept	
Review **Remember** and **Understand** levels		Unit 12
Apply Units 13–15	Carry out or use a procedure in a given situation	
generalize	draw conclusions based on presented information	Unit 13
infer	draw a logical conclusion using information or evidence	
use	apply a procedure to a task	
show	demonstrate an understanding of information	Unit 14
Review **Apply** level		Unit 15
Analyze Units 16–18	Break material into its constituent parts and determine how the parts relate to one another and to an overall structure or purpose	
distinguish	find differences that set one thing apart from another	Unit 16
select	choose from among alternatives	
arrange	organize information	Unit 17
organize	arrange in a systematic pattern	
outline	arrange information into a systematic pattern of main ideas and supporting details	
Review all levels		Unit 18
*The last two levels of Bloom's Taxonomy, **Evaluate** and **Create**, are covered in Book D.*		

Noun Form and Function (Units 1, 2, 3, 4, 7, 8, 9, and 11)

Form	Function
Adding the suffix **-s** to most singular nouns	makes a **plural noun**.
• map + s = maps • cab + s = cabs • mast + s = masts	• I had the **maps** at camp. • The **cabs** are fast. • The bats sat on the **masts**.
Adding the suffix **-es** to nouns ending in **s**, **z**, **x**, **ch**, **sh**, or **tch**	makes a **plural noun**.
• dress + es = dresses • fizz + es = fizzes • box + es = boxes • rich + es = riches • dish + es = dishes • match + es = matches	• Rose bought three new **dresses**. • They drank cherry **fizzes**. • The **boxes** were full of books. • The safe contains many **riches**. • The **dishes** fell to the floor. • The wet **matches** did not light.
Adding the suffix **-'s** to nouns	makes a **possessive singular noun**.
• Stan + 's = Stan's • van + 's = van's • man + 's = man's	• **Stan's** stamps are at camp. • The **van's** mat is flat. • The **man's** plan is to get clams.
Adding the suffix **-'s** to nouns	makes a **possessive plural noun**.
• boy + s' = boys' • girl + s' = girls' • dog+ s' = dogs'	• The **boys'** cards were missing. • The **girls'** snacks are on the table. • The **dogs'** bowls are empty.
Adding the **'** to a plural noun ending in **-es**	makes a **possessive plural noun**.
• foxes + ' = foxes' • fishes + ' = fishes'	• The **foxes'** den is snug. • The **fishes'** fins make waves.

Count Nouns—Nouns that can be specifically counted		
Rules	**Form**	**Examples**
• Can be preceded by the indefinite articles in the **singular** form	**a** **an**	a **bicycle**, a **cat**, a **table** an **insect**
• Can be made **plural**	**-s** **-es**	**bicycles, cats, tables, insects** **dresses, riches, suffixes**
• Can be preceded by the definite article in the **singular** form • Can be preceded by the definite article in the **plural** form when referring to specific objects, groups, or ideas	**the**	the **pencil**, the **pencils** the **insect**, the **insects** the **truck**, the **trucks**
• Can be preceded by the zero article (Ø) in the **plural** form	**zero article (Ø)**	(Ø) **Bicycles** are fun to ride. I see (Ø) **stars** in the sky. (Ø) **Insects** are not fun.
• Can be preceded by determiners in the **singular** form	**this**	This **bicycle** is red. This **lunch** is good. This **table** is round
	that	That **insect** is big. Do not light that **match**! That **truck** is running.
• Can be preceded by determiners in the **plural** form	**these** **those**	These **trucks** are red. Those **workers** are strong.
• Can be preceded by quantity adjectives **a lot of, any, many, some**, and **a few**	**a lot of** **any** **many** **some** **a few**	He has a lot of **friends**. I don't have any red **pencils**. She has many **cats**. I saw some **stars** in the sky. I need a few **paper clips**.
• Cannot be preceded by the quantity adjectives **much** or a **little**		**NOT:** She has much apples. There are a little stars in the sky.

Noun Form and Function (*continued*)

Noncount Nouns Cannot be specifically counted, but can be measured		
Rules	**Form**	**Examples**
• Can only be used in the singular form	singular	That was **fun**. The plant needs **water**. The pen is out of **ink**.
• Never take indefinite articles **a** and **an**		The room is filled with **smoke**. You need **cash** for the movie. I want **mustard** on my sandwich.
• Sometimes take the definite article **the**, if it refers to a specific object, group or idea.	**the**	Please pass me the **pasta**. The **soup** is on the table. Wash the **dirt** from your hands.
• Can be preceded by determiners **this** and **that**.	**this** **that**	This **corn** tastes great! That **water** looks dirty.
• Can be preceded by quantity adjectives **a lot of**, **any**, **much**, **some**, and **a little**.	**a lot of**	There is a lot of **mud** on the truck. I have a lot of **stuff**.
	any	This isn't any **fun**. I don't smell any **smoke**. Do you want any **rice**?
	much	This isn't much **fun**. That man has so much **hair**! Don't give me too much **jelly**.
	some	I want some **water**. Please pass me some **mustard**.
	a little	This popcorn needs a little **salt**. Please give me a little **pasta**.
• Cannot be preceded by the quantity adjectives **many**, and **a few**.		NOT: I have many stuff. She has a few cash.

Verb Form and Function (Units 4, 5, 7, 8, 10, 11,15, and 16)

Form	Function
Adding the suffix **-s** to most verbs ...	makes the verbs **third person singular**, **present tense**.
• sit + s = sits • skid + s = skids • pack + s = packs	• The rabbit **sits** in the grass. • The cab **skids** on the ramp. • She **packs** her bags for the trip.
Adding the suffix **-es** to verbs ending in **s**, **z**, **x**, **ch**, **sh**, or **tch**	makes the verbs **third person singular**, **present tense**.
• press + es = presses • buzz + es = buzzes • wax + es = waxes • switch + es = switches • wish + es = wishes • pitch + es = pitches	• He **presses** the button to open the door. • The bee **buzzes** around the room. • John **waxes** his car once a month. • She **switches** on the radio. • Jamal **wishes** he had a wagon. • Monica **pitches** her trash into the can.
Adding the suffix **-ed** to regular verbs	makes the **past tense**.
• jump + ed = jumped • smell + ed = smelled • end + ed = ended	• She **jumped**. • Stuart **smelled** the roses. • The class **ended** well.
Adding **will** before main verbs	makes the **future tense**.
• will + nap = will nap • will + send = will send • will + use = will use	• The baby **will nap** after lunch. • They **will send** it later. • Ron **will use** blue paint.

Verb Form and Function (*continued*)

Form	Function
Adding the suffix **-ing** to main verbs with the helping verb **am**, **is**, or **are**	makes the **present progressive**.
• go + ing = going • come + ing = coming • drop + ing = dropping	• I **am going** to the circus. • She **is coming** over to visit. • Leaves **are dropping** from the tree.
Adding the suffix **-ing** to main verbs with helping verbs **was** or **were**	makes the **past progressive**.
• push + ing = pushing • dump + ing = dumping • run + ing = running	• He **was pushing** the cart. • They **were dumping** sand into the water. • She **was running** down the street.
Adding the suffix **-ing** to main verbs with helping verbs **will be**	makes the **future progressive**.
• act + ing = acting • bring + ing = bringing • swim + ing = swimming	• I **will be acting** in the play. • She **will be bringing** her list. • They **will be swimming** at 6:00.

Form	Function
Adding the suffix **-ing** to verbs	forms a **present participle**, which can also act as an **adjective**.
• skid + ing = skidding • cry + ing = crying • migrate + ing = migrating	• The **skidding** car crashed into the tree. • I picked up the **crying** baby. • The **migrating** birds were high in the sky.
Adding the suffix **-ed** or **-en** to a verb	forms a **past participle**, which can also act as an **adjective**.
• hurry + ed = hurried • drive + en = driven	• The **hurried** effort did not help. • The **driven** athlete set new records.

Verb Forms (Units 4, 5, 7, 9, 10, and 11)

The Present Tense (Unit 4)

Person	Singular	Plural
First Person	I pass.	We pass.
Second Person	You pass.	You pass.
Third Person	He, she, it passes.	They pass.

The Past Tense (Unit 7)

Person	Singular	Plural
First Person	I passed.	We passed.
Second Person	You passed.	You passed.
Third Person	He, she, it passed.	They passed.

The Future Tense (Unit 10)

Person	Singular	Plural
First Person	I will pass.	We will pass.
Second Person	You will pass.	You will pass.
Third Person	He, she, it will pass.	They will pass.

The Present Progressive (Unit 5)

Person	Singular	Plural
First Person	I am sitting.	We are sitting.
Second Person	You are sitting.	You are sitting.
Third Person	He, she, it is sitting.	They sit.

The Past Progressive (Unit 9)

Person	Singular	Plural
First Person	I was passing.	We were passing.
Second Person	You were passing.	You were passing.
Third Person	He, she, it was passing.	They were passing.

The Future Progressive (Unit 11)

Person	Singular	Plural
First Person	I will be passing.	We will be passing.
Second Person	You will be passing.	You will be passing.
Third Person	He, she, it will be passing.	They will be passing.

Verb Forms (*continued*)

Forms of *Be, Have,* and *Do* (Units 13, 15, and 16)

Be	Present		Past		Future	
Person	Singular	Plural	Singular	Plural	Singular	Plural
First Person	I **am**	we **are**	I **was**	we **were**	I **will be**	we **will be**
Second Person	you **are**	you **are**	you **were**	you **were**	you **will be**	you **will be**
Third Person	he, she, it **is**	they **are**	he, she, it **was**	they **were**	he, she, it **will be**	they **will be**

Have	Present		Past		Future	
Person	Singular	Plural	Singular	Plural	Singular	Plural
First Person	I **have**	we **have**	I **had**	we **had**	I **will have**	we **will have**
Second Person	you **have**	you **have**	you **had**	you **had**	you **will have**	you **will have**
Third Person	he, she, it **has**	they **have**	he, she, it **had**	they **had**	he, she, it **will have**	they **will have**

Do	Present		Past		Future	
Person	Singular	Plural	Singular	Plural	Singular	Plural
First Person	I **do**	we **do**	I **did**	we **did**	I **will do**	we **will do**
Second Person	you **do**	you **do**	you **did**	you **did**	you **will do**	you **will do**
Third Person	he, she, it **does**	they **do**	he, she, it **did**	they **did**	he, she, it **will do**	they **will do**

Irregular Past Tense Verbs (Units 1–18)

Base Verb	Irregular Past Tense	Base Verb	Irregular Past Tense
be (am, is, are)	was/were	overtake	overtook
become	became	put	put
begin	began	ride	rode
bend	bent	ring	rang
bring	brought	rise	rose
catch	caught	run	ran
come	came	say	said
cost	cost	sell	sold
cut	cut	send	sent
dive	dove	shake	shook
do	did	shine	shone
drink	drank	sing	sang
drive	drove	sit	sat
fit	fit	spend	spent
fly	flew	spring	sprang
forget	forgot	stand	stood
forgive	forgave	stick	stuck
get	got	string	strung
give	gave	swim	swam
go	went	swing	swung
have	had	take	took
hit	hit	think	thought
know	knew	thrust	thrust
lend	lent	wake	woke
let	let	win	won
make	made	withstand	withstood
mistake	mistook	write	wrote
overcome	overcame		

Spelling Rules (Units 5, 6, 10, 15, and 17)

Rule	Examples
Words Ending With Double Letters	
At the end of one-syllable words, after a short vowel, / s /, / f /, / l /, and / z / are usually represented by double letters -**ss**, -**ff**, -**ll**, -**zz**.	• pa**ss** • blu**ff** • wi**ll** • ja**zz**
The Doubling Rule	
Double the final consonant before adding a suffix to a word when: • The word is one syllable. • The word has one vowel. • The word ends in one consonant.	• sip + ing = si**pp**ing • skid + ed = ski**dd**ed
Drop e Rule	
When adding a suffix that begins with a **vowel** to a **final silent e** word, drop the **e** from the base word. When adding a suffix that begins with a **consonant** to a **final silent e** word, do not drop the **e** from the base word.	• hope + ing = **hoping** • hope + ful = **hopeful**

Rule	Examples
Words Ending in <u>o</u>	
When a word ends in a consonant followed by <u>o</u>, form plural nouns and third person singular, present tense verbs by adding **-es**. Adding **-es** keeps the sound for <u>o</u> long.	• hero**es** • zero**es** • go**es**
When a word ends in a vowel followed by <u>o</u>, form the plural noun by adding **-s**.	• video**s**
Change <u>y</u> Rule	
When a base word ends in **y** preceded by a consonant, change **y** to **i** before adding a suffix, except for **-ing**.	• try + ed = tr**i**ed • try + ing = trying • happy + est = happ**i**est • happy + ness = happ**i**ness

Adjectives (Units 14, 15, and 17)

Adjective	Comparative
Adding the suffix **-er** to an adjective	compares one person, thing, or group to another person, thing, or group. The suffix **-er** means "more."
• fast + er = faster • small + er = smaller • big + er = bigger	• She is a **faster** runner than Sam. • Her backpack is **smaller** than my backpack. • That group of boys is **bigger** than this group of boys.

Adjective	Superlative
Adding the suffix **-est** to an adjective	compares one person, thing, or group to two or more persons, things, or groups. The suffix **-est** means "most."
• fast + est = fastest • small + est = smallest • big + est = biggest	• She is the **fastest** runner in school. • I got the **smallest** slice of pizza. • That gym has the **biggest** swimming pool of all.

Adjective	Adverb
Adding the suffix **-ly** to an adjective	changes the adjective to an adverb.
• glad + ly = gladly • final + ly = finally • perfect + ly = perfectly	• I **gladly** helped him cook the meal. • We **finally** got to the top of the hill. • She sang the song **perfectly**.

Prepositions (Unit 4)

about	as	by	into	since
above	at	down	like	than
across	before	during	near	to
after	behind	except	of	toward
against	below	for	off	under
along	beside	from	on	until
among	between	in	over	up
around	beyond	inside	past	with

Prefixes (Units 13–17)

Prefix	Meanings	Examples
anti-	against	antitoxin
con-	with	confirm
dis-	non; away, apart	distrust, distract
in-	in, into	inside, inflame
inter-	between, among	interact, interstate
non-	not, without	nonskid, nonsense
pre-	before	preregister
re-	back; again	return, review
sub-	below	subcontinent
super-	beyond	supersonic
trans-	across	transcontinental
un-	not, opposite	unlike, unhappy
under-	below	underfoot, underline

Idioms

Idioms (Units 1–18)

Idiom	Meaning
at the drop of a hat	immediately and without urging
be a live wire	be a vivacious, alert, or energetic person
be all wet	be entirely mistaken
be at sixes and sevens	be in a state of confusion or disorder
be at the end of your rope	be at the limit of one's patience, endurance, or resources
be beside yourself	be very concerned or worried
be down to the wire	be the very end, as in a race or contest
be fishy	cause doubt or suspicion
be in full swing	be at the highest level of activity
be in hot water	be in serious trouble or in an embarrassing situation with someone in authority
be in on the act	be included in an activity
be in the public eye	be frequently seen in public or in the media; be well-known
be in the red	be operating at a loss; in debt
be in the swim	active in the general current of affairs
be in the wind	likely to occur; in the offing
be like a fish out of water	appear completely out of place
be on the blink	be out of working order
be on the button	be exactly; precisely accurate
be on the rack	be under great stress
be on to	be aware of or have information about
be on your last leg	be unable to continue
be out of line	be uncalled for; improper; out of control
be out of your hands	be no longer within your responsibility or in your care
be out to lunch	not be in touch with the real world
be over the hill	be past the prime of life; be slowing down
be over the hump	be past the worst or most difficult part or stage

Idiom	Meaning
be the bottom line	be the final result or most crucial factor
be under the wire	be at the finish line; just in the nick of time; at the last moment
be up a creek	be in a difficult situation
be water over the dam	be something that is past and can't be changed
be within an inch of	be almost to the point of
bite the bullet	face a painful situation bravely and stoically
bite the dust	fall dead, especially in combat; be defeated; come to an end
call it quits	stop working or trying
call the shots	exercise authority; be in charge
call your bluff	challenge another with a display of strength or confidence
catch red-handed	catch someone in the act of doing something wrong
catch you in the act	catch you doing something illegal or private
catch you later	see or speak to you at a later time
come over to our side	join our group; take another position on the issue
come to life	become excited
come up smelling like a rose	result favorably or successfully
cost an arm and a leg	be high priced, though possibly not worth the cost
cover your tracks	hide evidence in order to dodge pursuers
cry your eyes out	weep inconsolably for a long time
do the trick	bring about the desired result
don't bug me	leave me alone
drive you crazy	make you angry, confused, or frustrated
fill the bill	serve a particular purpose
get down to brass tacks	begin talking about important things; get down to business
get it off your chest	let go of your pent-up feelings
get off your back	have someone stop bothering you

Idiom	Meaning
get on the stick	begin to work
get on your nerves	irritate or exasperate you
get ripped off	be taken advantage of
get the ax	get fired
get the short end of the stick	get the worst of an unequal deal
get up on the wrong side of bed	be in a really bad mood
give it your best shot	try as hard as you can to accomplish something
give me a ring	phone me
give someone the shirt off your back	be extremely generous
go along for the ride	join an activity for no particular reason
go down the tubes	fall into a state of failure or ruin
go fly a kite	go away or stop annoying someone (usually said in anger)
go to bat for	give help to; defend
go to the dogs	decline, come to a bad end
go up in flames	be utterly destroyed
go up in smoke	be totally destroyed
have a bone to pick	have grounds for a complaint or dispute
have a leg to stand on	have a good defense for your opinions or actions
have cabin fever	feel uneasiness or distress because of being in an enclosed space
have you in stitches	have you laughing uncontrollably
have your fingers crossed	hope for a successful or advantageous outcome
hit close to home	affect your feelings or interests
hit the deck	get out of bed; fall or drop to a prone position; prepare for action
hit the jackpot	win; have success
hit the sack	go to bed

Idiom	Meaning
hit the spot	be exactly right
hold your horses	slow down; wait a minute; be patient
kick the habit	free oneself from addiction, as cigarettes
lend a hand	help someone
let the cat out of the bag	let a secret be known
look down your nose at	regard with contempt or condescension
look up to	admire
make a dent in	get started with a series of chores
make a drop in the bucket	make an insufficient or inconsequential amount in comparison to what is required
make no bones about	be forthright and candid about; acknowledge freely
make the grade	measure up to a given standard
make tracks	move or leave in a hurry
make waves	cause a disturbance or controversy
open your eyes	become aware of the truth of a situation
pass the buck	shift responsibility or blame to another person
pass the hat	take up a collection of money
pat on the back	congratulate; encourage someone
pull a fast one	play a trick or carry out a fraud
pull the rug out from under you	remove all support and help from you
pull your leg	kid, fool, or trick you
push your luck	expect continued good fortune
put all your eggs in one basket	risk everything all at once
put the cart before the horse	do things out of order; not do things logically
put to bed	make final preparations for completing a project
put two and two together	draw the proper conclusions from existing evidence or indications

Idiom	Meaning
put your finger on something	point out or describe exactly; find something
ring a bell	arouse an indistinct memory
rub your nose in it	remind you of something unfortunate that has happened
run like clockwork	operate with machinelike regularity and precision; perfectly
run out of gas	exhaust your energy or enthusiasm
saved by the bell	rescued from a difficult situation just in time
see eye-to-eye	be in agreement
send someone packing	dismiss someone abruptly
shake a leg	hurry
sink or swim	fail or succeed on your own
snap out of it	go back to your normal condition from depression, grief, or self-pity
stack the deck	order things against someone
stick your neck out	take a risk
strike it rich	gain sudden financial success
stuck in a rut	staying in a way of living that never changes
take a hike	leave because your presence is unwanted
take a shot in the dark	take a wild guess; an attempt that has little chance of succeeding
take a stand	take an active role in demonstrating your belief in something
take an eye for an eye	permit an offender to suffer what a victim has suffered
take at your word	be convinced of your sincerity and act in accord with what you say
take five	take a short rest or break, as of five or ten minutes
take it from the top	start from the beginning
take the bull by the horns	deal with a problem directly and resolutely

Idiom	Meaning
take the cake	be the most outrageous or disappointing; win the prize; be outstanding
the sky is the limit	have no limit to what you can spend, how far you can go, or what you can achieve
tilt at windmills	confront and engage in conflict with an imagined opponent or threat
turn your back on	deny; reject; abandon; foresake
(when) push comes to shove	when the situation becomes more difficult or matters escalate
win by a landslide	get the most of the votes in an election
wing it	go through a situation or process without any plan
work like a dog	work very hard
work your fingers to the bone	labor extremely hard; toil

Glossary of Terms

Books A, B, and C include these terms. Unit numbers following each definition indicate where these terms first appear.

Adjective. A word used to describe a noun. An adjective tells which one, how many, or what kind. A prepositional phrase may also be used as an adjective. Example: *The quick team from the school won the game.* (Unit 6)

Adjective, possessive. A word that comes before a noun and is used to describe the noun in terms of possession. Examples: *my, your, his, her, its, our, their. My desk is messy.* (Unit 7)

Adverb. A word used to describe a verb, an adjective, or another adverb. An adverb answers the questions *when, where,* or *how.* A prepositional phrase may also be used as an adverb. Examples: *He ran yesterday. She hopped in the grass. He batted quickly.* (Unit 4)

Antonym. A word that means the opposite of another word. Examples: *good/bad; fast/slow; happy/sad.* (Unit 2)

Apostrophe. A punctuation mark used in possessive singular and plural nouns. Examples: *Fran's hat, the boys' cards.* It is also used in contractions. Examples: isn't, can't. (Units 2, 7)

Attribute. A characteristic or quality, such as size, part, color, or function. Examples: *She lost the big stamp. Fish have gills. He has a green truck. A clock tells time.* (Unit 5)

Base Verb. The form of a verb without any suffixes; the infinitive form without *to.* Examples: *be, help, spell.* (Unit 7)

Biography. A type of literature that tells the story of someone's life. Example: *"Leonardo da Vinci: The Inventor."* (Unit 13)

Comma. A punctuation mark used to signal a pause when reading or writing to clarify meaning. Example: *Due to snow, school was cancelled.* (Unit 5)

Command. A sentence that makes a request. Example: *Show the parts of the invention.* (Unit 13)

Compound word. A word made up of two or more smaller words. Examples: *backdrop, hilltop.* (Unit 3)

Conjunction. A function word that joins words, phrases, or clauses in a sentence or across two sentences. Examples: *and, but, or.* (Unit 7)

Consonant. A closed speech sound in which the airflow is restricted or closed by the lips, teeth, or tongue. Letters represent consonant sounds. Examples: <u>m</u>, <u>r</u>, <u>g</u>, <u>w</u>, <u>q</u>. (Unit 1)

Consonant blend. Consonant sound pair in the same syllable. The consonants are not separated by vowels. Initial blends are letter combinations that represent two different consonant sounds at the beginning of a word. Examples: **bl**ack, **br**im, **sk**ill, **tw**in. Final blends are letter pairs that represent two different consonant sounds at the end of a word. Examples: bu**mp**, se**nd**, la**st**. (Unit 11)

Consonant cluster. Three or more consecutive consonants in the same syllable. Examples: <u>scr</u>, <u>spl</u>. (Unit 11)

Contraction. Two words combined into one word. Some letters are left out and are replaced by an apostrophe. Examples: *isn't, can't, I'd*. (Unit 7)

Digraph. Two-letter grapheme that represents one sound. Examples: <u>ch</u>, <u>sh</u>, <u>th</u>. (Unit 8)

Direct object. A noun or pronoun that receives the action of the main verb in the predicate. It answers the question: Who or what received the action? Examples: *Casey hit the **ball**. She dropped the **mitt***. (Unit 3)

Direct object, compound. Two direct objects joined by a conjunction in a sentence. Example: *The bugs infest **crops and animals***. (Unit 9)

Doubling rule. A spelling rule in English that doubles a final consonant before adding a suffix beginning with a vowel when 1) a one-syllable word 2) with one vowel 3) ends in one consonant. Examples: *hopping, robbed*. (Unit 6)

Drama. A story, such as a play, musical, or opera, written for characters to act out. Example: **"These Shoes of Mine."** (Unit 15)

Expository text. Text that provides information and includes a topic. Facts and examples support the topic. Example: **"What Is Jazz?"** (Unit 5)

Expression. A common way of saying something. An expression is similar to an **idiom**. Example: *all wet* means "mistaken; on the wrong track." (Unit 7)

First-person account. A type of writing, either fiction or nonfiction, in which the narrator recalls personal experiences. Example: **"A. H. Gardiner's Account"** in **"King Tut: Egyptian Pharaoh."** (Unit 17)

Genre. A literary category. Examples of genres include: biography, fiction, folktale, nonfiction, science fiction, and short story. (Unit 13)

Homophones. Words that sound the same but have different meanings. Examples: *son/sun; some/sum; one/won.* (Unit 7)

Idiom. A common phrase that cannot be understood by the meanings of its separate words—only by the entire phrase. Example: *be in the wind* means "likely to occur." (Unit 4)

Indirect object. A noun or pronoun often placed between the main verb and the direct object. It tells to whom or for whom the action was done. Example: *The king offered his **son** a gift.* (Unit 17)

Metaphor. A figure of speech that compares people, places, things, or feelings without using the words *like* or *as.* Examples: *He is a **prince**. Her **sunny** smile.* (Unit 14)

Mood. A literary device that conveys a general emotion of a work or an author. Example: **"The First Transcontinental Railroad"** uses mood as a literary device. (Unit 18)

Myth. An anonymous tale based on the traditional beliefs of a culture that often includes supernatural beings and heroes. Example: **"Legendary Superheroes."** (Unit 15)

Narrative text. Text that tells a story. A story has characters, settings, events, conflict, and a resolution.

Example: **"Atlas: The Book of Maps."** (Unit 2)

Noun. A word that names a person, place, thing, or idea. Examples: *teacher, city, bat, peace.* (Unit 1)

Noun, abstract. A word that names an idea or a thought that we cannot see or touch. Examples: *love, Saturday, sports, democracy.* (Unit 3)

Noun, common. A word that names a general person, place, or thing. Examples: *man, city, statue.* (Unit 3)

Noun, concrete. A word that names a person, place, or thing that we can see or touch. Examples: *teacher, city, pencil.* (Unit 3)

Noun, proper. A word that names a specific person, place, or thing. Examples: *Mr. West, Boston, Statue of Liberty.* (Unit 3)

Onomatopoeia. A literary device created when a word's sound suggests its meaning. Examples: *crash, bang, zip.* (Unit 16)

Open syllable. A syllable ending with a vowel sound. Examples: *go, be, pay.* (Unit 15)

Past participle. The **-ed** or **-en** form of a verb. It can act as an adjective to describe a noun. Examples: *Traffic clogged the **divided** highway. The **driven** athlete set new records.* (Unit 16)

Personification. Figurative language that assigns human characteristics to an animal, idea, or a thing. Example: **"Roberto Clemente: The Heart of the Diamond."** (Unit 16)

Phrase. A group of words that does the same job as a single word. Examples: *at lunch, in the park, to stay in shape.* (Unit 4)

Plural. A term that means "more than one." In English, nouns are made plural by adding **-s** or **-es**. Examples: *figs, backpacks, dresses.* (Unit 1)

Predicate. One of two main parts of an English sentence. It includes the main verb of the sentence. Examples: *He **digs**. She **lost the big stamp**.* (Unit 2)

Predicate, complete. The verb and all of its modifiers in a sentence. Example: *The class **clapped during the song**.* (Unit 8)

Predicate, compound. Two or more verbs joined by a conjunction. Example: *The class **sang and clapped**.* (Unit 8)

Predicate, simple. The verb in a sentence. Example: *The class **clapped** during the song.* (Unit 8)

Prefix. A morpheme added to the beginning of a word to modify its meaning. Examples: **mis**interpret, **non**stop, **un**plug (Unit 13)

Preposition. A function word that begins a prepositional phrase. Examples: *at, from, in.* (Unit 4)

Prepositional phrase. A phrase that begins with a preposition and ends with a noun or a pronoun. A prepositional phrase is used either as an adjective or as an adverb. Examples: *at the track, from the old map, in traffic.* (Unit 4)

Present participle. The -ing verb form that expresses present action. It follows a helping verb, such as *am, is, are*. The **-ing** forms of verbs can also act as adjectives to describe nouns Examples: *She **is coming** to the picnic. The **running** water spilled on the floor.* (Units 5, 15)

Progressive. A verb form that indicates ongoing action in time. Examples: *I **am going*** (present); *I **was going*** (past); *I **will be going*** (future). (Units 5, 9, 11)

Pronoun. A function word used in place of a noun. Pronouns can be subject, object, or possessive. (Units 4, 6, 7)

Pronoun, object. A pronoun that takes the place of the object in a sentence. Example: *Jason threw **it**.* (Unit 7)

Pronoun, possessive. A pronoun that shows possession. Examples: *mine, yours, his, hers, ours, theirs. Mary's desk is neat. **Mine** is messy.* (Unit 7)

Pronoun, subject. A pronoun that takes the place of the subject in a sentence. Also called a nominative pronoun. Example: ***He** ran down the street.* (Unit 7)

R-controlled syllable. A syllable that contains a vowel followed by **r**. Examples: *her, far, sport.* (Unit 14)

Schwa. A vowel phoneme in an unstressed syllable that has reduced value or emphasis. The symbol for schwa is ə. Example: *across (ə-krŏs′).* (Unit 13)

Science fiction. A type of literature that features a setting and people that are futuristic or fantastic. Example: **"Podway Bound: A Science Fiction Story."** (Unit 13)

Sentence. A group of words that has at least one subject and one predicate and conveys a complete thought. Examples: *She ran. The map is in the cab.* (Unit 1)

Sentence, simple. A group of words that has one subject and one predicate and conveys a complete thought. Example: *The man ran fast.* (Unit 2)

Simile. A figure of speech that makes a comparison. A simile always uses the words "like" or "as." Examples: *He runs **like the wind**. Her dreams are **as** big **as the ocean**.* (Unit 14)

Statement. A sentence that presents a fact or opinion. Examples: *The map is flat. The twins are remarkable.* (Unit 2)

Story. An account of events. A story has characters, setting, events, a conflict, and a resolution. Example: **"Floki, Sailor Without a Map."** (Unit 2)

Stress. The emphasis that a syllable has in a word. Examples: *atlas (at'ləs), across (ə-krŏs′).* (Unit 13)

Subject. One of two main parts of an English sentence. The subject names the person, place, thing, or idea that the sentence is about. Examples: ***She** raps. **Boston** digs.* (Unit 2)

Subject, complete. A subject (noun or pronoun) and all of its modifiers. Example: ***The blue egg** fell from the nest.* (Unit 7)

Subject, compound. A subject that consists of two or more nouns or pronouns joined by a conjunction. Example: ***Ellen and her class** passed.* (Unit 7)

Subject, simple. The noun or pronoun that is the subject of a sentence. Example: *The **bird** sings. The blue **egg** fell from the nest.* (Unit 7)

Suffix. A word ending that modifies a word's meaning. Examples: ***-ing**, **-ed**, **-ly**.* (Unit 17)

Syllable. A word or word part that has one vowel sound. Examples: *bat, dig, tox-ic, pic-nic.* (Unit 3)

Symbol. An image, figure, or object that represents a different thing or idea. Example: *In ancient Egypt, a pyramid is a **symbol** of the creation mound.* (Unit 17)

Synonym. A word that has the same or a similar meaning to another word. Examples: *big/huge, quick/fast, fix/repair.* (Unit 3)

Tense. Changes in the form of a verb that show changes in time: present, past, or future. Examples: *act, acted, will act.* (Units 4, 7, 10)

Trigraph. A three-letter grapheme that represents one sound. Example: **-tch** (wa**tch**). (Unit 8)

Verb. A word that describes an action (*run, make*) or a state of being (*is, were*) and shows time. Examples: *acts* (present tense, happening now); *is dropping* (present progressive, ongoing action); *acted* (past tense, happened in the past); *will act* (future tense, will happen in the future). (Units 4, 5, 7, 10)

Verb, helping. An auxiliary verb that precedes the main verb in a sentence. Helping verbs include forms of *be, do,* and *have.* (Unit 11)

Verb phrase. A group of words that does the job of a verb, conveys tense, and has two parts, which are the helping verb and the main verb. Example: *The bus **is stopping**.* (Unit 9)

Vowel. A speech sound in which the airflow is open. Letters represent vowel sounds. Examples: <u>a</u>, <u>e</u>, <u>i</u>, <u>o</u>, <u>u</u>, and sometimes <u>y</u>. (Unit 1)

Sources

Unit 13

Off-the-Wall Inventions, Solving Problems, It'll Never Work

Griffiths, Nick. 1995. "It'll Never Work," from *Young Telegraph: Incredible Inventions*. London: Two-Can Publishing Ltd. © 1995 by Two-Can Publishing, an imprint of Creative Publishing International, Inc. Adapted by permission of Creative Publishing International, Inc.

Way to Go!

Miller, Steve. 1998. "Way to Go," from *Odyssey* (May), vol. 7, no. 5. Carus Publishing Company, 315 Fifth Street, Peru, IL 61354. All rights reserved. Adapted with permission.

Leonardo da Vinci: The Inventor

D'Alto, Nick. 2001. "From the Notebooks of Leonardo," from *Odyssey* (November), vol. 10, no. 8. Carus Publishing Company, 315 Fifth Street, Peru, IL 61354. All rights reserved. Adapted with permission.

Kralik, Milan, Jr. 2002. "Leonardo's Notebooks," from *Calliope* (March), vol. 12, no. 7. Carus Publishing Company, 315 Fifth Street, Peru, IL 61354. All rights reserved. Adapted with permission.

Museum of Science, Boston. 2003. "Leonardo da Vinci: Scientist, Inventor, Artist," from the website of the *Museum of Science*, Boston. http://www.mos.org/ leonardo/inventor.html (accessed November 1, 2004).

Podway Bound: A Science Fiction Story

Werfel, Justin. 1998. "Podway Bound," from *Odyssey* (May), vol. 7, no. 5. Carus Publishing Company, 315 Fifth Street, Peru, IL 61354. All rights reserved. Adapted with permission.

Unit 14

Making Art

Crandall, Sally. 2002. "Comic Book Artist at Work," from *AppleSeeds* (May), vol. 4, no. 9. Carus Publishing Company, 315 Fifth Street, Peru, IL 61354. All rights reserved. Adapted with permission.

Art at Home and Art in Caves

Newman, Patricia M. 2002. "Elisa Kleven: From Scraps to Magic," from *AppleSeeds* (May), vol. 4, no. 9. Carus Publishing Company, 315 Fifth Street, Peru, IL 61354. All rights reserved. Adapted with permission.

From Rock Art to Graffiti

Bahn, Paul G. 2001. "The Start of Art," from *Dig* (November/December), vol. 3, no. 5. Carus Publishing Company, 315 Fifth Street, Peru, IL 61354. All rights reserved. Adapted with permission.

Gingold, Craig. 1989. "The Murals of Aztlán," from *Cobblestone* (April), vol.10, no. 4. Carus Publishing Company, 315 Fifth Street, Peru, IL 61354. All rights reserved. Adapted with permission.

Estate of Keith Haring. 2003. from Biography section of the *Keith Haring website*. http://www.haring.com/master_ bio.htm (accessed November 1, 2004).

Gruen, John. 2002. "Keith Haring: A Biography for Children," from *Haring Kids* website. Keith Haring Foundation. http:// www.haringkids.com/master_k_life.htm (accessed November 1, 2004).

Becoming an Artist

Wild, Patricia. 2002. "Famous Artists' Beginnings," from *AppleSeeds* (May), vol. 4, no. 9. Carus Publishing Company, 315 Fifth Street, Peru, IL 61354. All rights reserved. Adapted with permission.

National Endowment for the Humanities Seminar of Kenyon College. 1997–98. "Augusta Savage," from the website of Kenyon College, Gambier, Ohio. http://northbysouth.kenyon.edu/1998/art/pages/savage.htm (accessed November 1, 2004).

Greene, Louise L. 2002. "Action Artist," from *AppleSeeds* (May), vol. 4, no. 9. Carus Publishing Company, 315 Fifth Street, Peru, IL 61354. All rights reserved. Adapted with permission.

Newman, Patricia M. 2002. "Elisa Kleven: From Scraps to Magic," from *AppleSeeds* (May), vol. 4, no. 9. Carus Publishing Company, 315 Fifth Street, Peru, IL 61354. All rights reserved. Adapted with permission.

Crandall, Sally. 2002. "Comic Book Artist at Work," from *AppleSeeds* (May), vol. 4, no. 9. Carus Publishing Company, 315 Fifth Street, Peru, IL 61354. All rights reserved. Adapted with permission.

Leonardo the Artist

Balch, Katherine S. 2001. "Leonardo: Engineer, Anatomist, Painter...Magician?" from *Odyssey* (November), vol. 10, no. 8. Carus Publishing Company, 315 Fifth Street, Peru, IL 61354. All rights reserved. Adapted with permission.

Budd, Denise. 2002. "The Master Works," from *Calliope* (March), vol.12, no. 7. Carus Publishing Company, 315 Fifth Street, Peru, IL 61354. All rights reserved. Adapted with permission.

Museum of Science, Boston. 2003. "Leonardo da Vinci: Scientist, Inventor, Artist," from the website of the *Museum of Science*, Boston. http://www.mos.org/leonardo/artist.html (accessed November 1, 2004).

Art in Space

Malina, Roger. 1999. "Space(y) Art," from *Odyssey* (November), vol. 8, no. 8. Carus Publishing Company, 315 Fifth Street, Peru, IL 61354. All rights reserved. Adapted with permission.

Pietronigro, Frank. 2004. "Frank Pietronigro: Interdisciplinary Fine Artist." from the homepage of Frank Pietronigro. http://www.pietronigro.com/index.htm (accessed November 1, 2004).

Unit 15

Mythical Heroes

Columbia Encyclopedia (Sixth ed.). 2001–2004. New York: Columbia University Press. www.bartleby.com; http://www.loggia.com/myth/pantheon.html (accessed November 1, 2004).

Legendary Superheroes

Watts, Claire, and Robert Nicholson. 1995. *Info Adventure: Super Heroes*. London: Two-Can Publishing Ltd., an imprint of Creative Publishing International, Inc. Adapted by permission of Creative Publishing International, Inc.

These Shoes of Mine

Soto, Gary. 1999. "These Shoes of Mine," play © 1999 by Gary Soto. Used with permission of the author and BookStop Literary Agency.

Navajo Code Talkers

Cluff, Nancy E. 2003. "Top Secret: An Interview with Sam Billison, Navajo Code Talker," from *AppleSeeds* (March), vol. 5, no. 7. Carus Publishing Company, 315 Fifth Street, Peru, IL 61354. All rights reserved. Adapted with permission.

Watson, Bruce. 1999. "Human Code Machine," from *Odyssey* (January), vol. 8, no. 1. Carus Publishing Company, 315 Fifth Street, Peru, IL 61354. All rights reserved. Adapted with permission.

The Ride of Her Life

Andrews, Rose. 1998. "The Ride of Her Life," from *AppleSeeds* (September), vol. 1, no. 1. Carus Publishing Company, 315 Fifth Street, Peru, IL 61354. All rights reserved. Adapted with permission.

Unit 16

The Complete Athlete, A Special Kind of Athlete

Crooker, Gary. 2003. "The Special Olympics," from *Faces* (September), vol. 20, no. 1. Carus Publishing Company, 315 Fifth Street, Peru, IL 61354. All rights reserved. Adapted with permission.

Hellickson, A.J. 2004. "Marathon Madness," from scholastic.com. Copyright © 2004 by Scholastic Inc. Reprinted with permission of Scholastic Inc. http://teacher.scholastic.com/scholasticnews/indepth/special_olympics/athletes/index.asp?article=stevenwalker.

Tony Hawk: Extreme Athlete

Tony Hawk, Inc. 2003. Biography from the *Tony Hawk's Official Website*. Tony Hawk, Inc. http://www.tonyhawk.com/bio.cfm (accessed November 1, 2004).

Swifter, Higher, Stronger

Stalcup, Ann. 2000. "Swifter, Higher, Stronger," from *Faces* (September), vol. 17, no. 1. Carus Publishing Company, 315 Fifth Street, Peru, IL 61354. All rights reserved. Adapted with permission.

Roberto Clemente: The Heart of the Diamond

Blair, Matthew K. 2003. "Roberto Clemente: The Greatest Right-Fielder Ever to Play the Game of Baseball," from the website, http://www.toptown.com/hp/66/roberto.htm (accessed November 1, 2004).

Loftus, Joanne. 1989. "The Heart of the Diamond," from *Cobblestone* (April), vol. 10, no. 4. Carus Publishing Company, 315 Fifth Street, Peru, IL 61354. All rights reserved. Adapted with permission.

Unit 17

The Pyramids, Building a Pyramid

Ayad, Mariam. 2001. "Building a Pyramid," from *Calliope* (September), vol. 12, no. 1. Carus Publishing Company, 315 Fifth Street, Peru, IL 61354. All rights reserved. Adapted with permission.

Living in Egypt, Growing Up Egyptian

Haynes, Joyce. 1999. "School Days," from *AppleSeeds* (February), vol. 1, no. 6. Carus Publishing Company, 315 Fifth Street, Peru, IL 61354. All rights reserved. Adapted with permission.

Wymore, Peggy Wilgus. 1999. "Growing Up in Another Time, Another Place," from *AppleSeeds* (February), vol. 1, no. 6. Carus Publishing Company, 315 Fifth Street, Peru, IL 61354. All rights reserved. Adapted with permission.

The Study of Mummies

Haynes, Joyce. 1997. "The Story of the Manchester Museum Mummies," from *Calliope* (September), vol. 8, no. 1. Carus Publishing Company, 315 Fifth Street, Peru, IL 61354. All rights reserved. Adapted with permission.

King Tut: Egyptian Pharaoh

Malek, Jaromir, ed. 2002. "A.H. Gardiner's account of the opening of the burial chamber of Tutankhamen on February 16, 1923." From the *Archive of the Griffith Institute*. Oxford: Griffith Institute.

Scherer, Jane, and Susan Washburn.
1999. "The Boy King," from *AppleSeeds*
(February), vol. 1, no. 6. Carus Publishing
Company, 315 Fifth Street, Peru, IL
61354. All rights reserved. Adapted
with permission.

Unit 18

Life at the Pole, Mysteries of Antarctica

Lewis, Karen E. 2001. "Mysteries of
Antarctica," from *AppleSeeds* (February),
vol. 3, no. 6. Carus Publishing Company,
315 Fifth Street, Peru, IL 61354. All rights
reserved. Adapted with permission.

The First Transcontinental Railroad

Gemmell, Charlotte. 1980. "The Builders
of the First Transcontinental Railroad,"
from *Cobblestone* (May), vol. 1, no. 5.
Carus Publishing Company, 315 Fifth
Street, Peru, IL 61354. All rights
reserved. Adapted with permission.

Continental Drift

Ammar, Hanan. 2003. "Continental
Drift," from *The Learning Haven website*.
Adapted with permission of Hanan
Ammar at LearningHaven.com. http://
www.funsocialstudies.learninghaven.
com/articles/conddrft1.htm (accessed
November 1, 2004).

Noyes-Hull, Gretchen. 1999. "Seashells
on the Summit," from *Appleseeds*
(October), vol. 2, no. 2. Carus Publishing
Company, 315 Fifth Street, Peru, IL
61354. All rights reserved. Adapted with
permission.

Reina, Mary. 2001. "The Pangea Puzzle,"
from *Appleseeds* (February) vol. 3, no. 6.
Carus Publishing Company, 315 Fifth
Street, Peru, IL 61354. All rights
reserved. Adapted with permission.

The Quest for a Continent

Weston, Beth. 1992. "A Stranger to
Foreign Shores," from *Cobblestone*
(January), vol. 13, no. 1. Carus Publishing
Company, 315 Fifth Street, Peru, IL
61354. All rights reserved. Adapted with
permission.

Word Histories

American Heritage Dictionary (Fourth
ed.). 2002. Boston: Houghton Mifflin Co.
http://www.bartleby.com/61/ (accessed
November 1, 2004).

Photo and Illustration Credits

Cover

Illustration

©Martin French/Morgan Gaynin Inc.

Unit 13

Photographs

16: www.sinclairc5.com. 18: Royalty Free©Digital Vision. 19: ©Hulton-Deutsch Collection/Corbis. 20: Purdue News Service Photo by Nick Judy. 21: Courtesy of DaimlerChrysler Corporation. 21: *bkgd.* Dennis O'Clair/GettyImages. 22–23: *Hovercraft.* Courtesy of Andreas Gronarz. 24: Courtesy of the Denver Post. 28: Giuseppe Cacace/Getty Images.

Illustrations

1, 16–17: Steve Clark. 25–26: Phaidon Press/©2004 Jupiter Images. 27: Time Life Pictures/Getty Images. 29–34: Ivan Velez.

Unit 14

Photographs

52: Elisa Kleven 56: *top.* ©Bettmann/Corbis. 60: top. Photograph ©Morgan & Marvin Smith/Schomburg Center. 60: *bottom.* ©Owaki-Kulla/Corbis. 70–71: insets. NASA. 70–73: *earth.* NASA. 72: *inset.* www.pietronigro.com/NASA. 73: *inset.* www.pietronigro.com/NASA.

Illustrations

35: ©2004 Dynamic Graphics. 50–51: ©2004 Jupiter Images. 53: From *The Lion and the Little Red Bird* by Elisa Kleven, ©1992 by Elisa Kleven. Used by Permission of Dutton Children's Books, A Division of Penguin Young Readers Group, A Member of Penguin Group (USA) Inc., 345 Hudson Street, New York, NY 10014. All rights reserved. 54: ©Fotosearch Stock Photography. 55: ©2004 Dynamics Graphics. 56: *bottom.* Schalkwijk/Art Resource, NY. 57: © The Estate of Keith Haring. 59: *easel.* Becky Malone. 62: ©Keron Grant/Marvel Comics. 63–68: Phaidon Press©2004 Jupiter Images.

Unit 15

Photographs

75: ©1999–2004 Getty Images. 90: Scala/ Art Resource, NY. 91: Royalty Free Creatas, NASA, Royalty Free Thinkstock, Royalty Free Photodisc, Royalty Free Thinkstock. 104: Photograph No. (NARA, 127-N-69889B);(Ashman); Official U.S. Marine Corps Photo USMC #57875. 108: ©United States Mint. Courtesy of Jeannie Sandoval. 114: Courtesy of Putnam County Historian.

Illustrations

92: Steve Clark. 93–94: ©2004 Jupiter Images. 95: ©Jonathon Earl Bowser-www.JonathonArt.com. 96, 99–100, 102. Laura Lacamara. 104–109: *map.* Reproduced from *Natural Advanced Geography.* America Book Co., e. 1898, 1901. Public Domain. 110–113: Courtesy of Mark Mitchell. 112: ©United States Postal Service.

Unit 16

Photographs

130: ©Jonathan Nourok/PhotoEdit. 131: ©Icon Sports Media/Tony Donaldson. 132: ©Jonathan Nourok/PhotoEdit. 134: Ray Ryan/SPORTSFILE *EDI*. 136–137, 139: Courtesy of THI. 143: ©Tami Chappell/Reuters/Corbis. 144: Courtesy of Carnegie Library of Pittsburgh. 144: bkgd. ©ArtVision. 146: ©Bettmann/Corbis. 147: ©ArtVision. 148: Courtesy of Carnegie Library of Pittsburgh.

Illustrations

115: Martin French. 130, 135–136, 140: Steve Clark. 141: ©Rykoff Collection/Corbis. 142, 145, 148: Steve Clark.

Unit 17

Photographs

164: top. ©Picturequest LLC 1998-2003. 166: *inset.* Will & Deni McIntyre/GettyImages. 169: ©Corel Corporation 1995. 170: ©The Granger Collection, New York. 172: ©2004 Jupiter Images. 173: The Minneapolis Institute of Arts, The William Hood Dunwoody Fund. 175–175: ©The Manchester Museum, The University of Manchester. 178: ©Royalty Free/Corbis., ©Roger Wood/Corbis, 1998-2004 Picturequest LLC. 180: ©Royalty Free/Corbis. 184: ©Royalty Free/Corbis.

Illustrations

149: www.mapresources.com. 164–165: Steve Clark. 166–168: Steve Clark. 171: University of Pennsylvania. 173: *bottom.* Steve Clark. 181: Becky Malone.

Unit 18

Photographs

185: ©2004 PictureArts Corporation. 202: ©1999-2004 Getty Images. 203: Courtesy of National Oceanic & Atmospheric Administration/ Department of Commerce. 204: ©1999-2004 Getty Images. 205: ©U.S. Coast Guard Slide. 206: *top.* Courtesy of The Antarctic Meteorite Laboratory at the Johnson Space Center. 206: ©Sky Valley Pictures. 207, 209: Courtesy of Pacific Railroad History Museum, ©2004, CPRR.org. 210: Shuji Maeda 211: ©Royalty Free/Corbis.

Illustrations

207: *map.* Courtesy of Pacific Railroad History Museum, ©2004, CPRR.org. 212: Courtesy of Pacific Railroad History Museum, ©2004, CPRR.org. 213–214: Courtesy of Pacific Railroad History Museum, ©2004, CPRR.org. 215: ©North Wind Picture Archives. 216: ©2004 Jupiter Images. 217: ©North Wind Picture Archives.